D0615875

PHUKET
ENCOUNTER

ADAM SKOLNICK

Phuket Encounter

Published by Lonely Planet Publications Pty Ltd
ABN 36 005 607 983

Australia	Head Office, Locked Bag 1, Footscray,
	Vic 3011
	☎ 03 8379 8000 fax 03 8379 8111
	talk2us@lonelyplanet.com.au
USA	150 Linden St, Oakland, CA 94607
	☎ 510 250 6400
	toll free 800 275 8555
	fax 510 893 8572
	info@lonelyplanet.com
UK	2nd fl, 186 City Rd
	London EC1V 2NT
	☎ 020 7106 2100 fax 020 7106 2101
	go@lonelyplanet.co.uk

This title was commissioned in Lonely Planet's
Melbourne office and produced by: **Commissioning
Editor** Carolyn Boicos **Coordinating Editors** Kristin
Odijk, Simon Williamson **Coordinating Cartographer**
Peter Shields **Assisting Cartographer** Amanda Sierp
Layout Designer Paul Iacono **Senior Editor** Katie
Lynch **Managing Cartographer** David Connolly **Cover
Designer** Pepi Bluck **Project Managers** Glenn van der
Knijff, Chris Love **Series Designers** Mik Ruff, Wendy
Wright **Managing Layout Designer** Adam McCrow
Thanks to Glenn Beanland, Ryan Evans, Quentin Frayne,
Nicole Hansen, Laura Jane, Naomi Parker, Celia Wood

Cover photograph Phuket, Thailand, Photolibrary
Angelo Cavalli/Superstock **Internal photographs** p99
by A Skolnick; p21 Roger Cracknell/Alamy; p25 Kevin
R Morris/Corbis; p130 FAN travelstock/Alamy; p143
ImageState/Alamy; p150 Yvan Cohen/OnAsia. All other
photographs by Lonely Planet Images, and by Austin Bush
except p22 Anders Blomqvist; p133 Andrew Bain; p137
Holger Leue; p5 Joe Cummings; p135 John Borthwick; p26
Kraig Lieb; p28 Paul Beinssen.

All images are copyright of the photographers unless
otherwise indicated. Many of the images in this guide
are available for licensing from **Lonely Planet Images:**
www.lonelyplanetimages.com.

ISBN 9781741049145

Printed through Colorcraft Ltd, Hong Kong.
Printed in China.

HOW TO USE THIS BOOK
Colour-Coding & Maps
Colour-coding is used for symbols on maps and in
the text that they relate to (eg all eating venues on
the maps and in the text are given a green knife and
fork symbol). Each neighbourhood also gets its own
colour, and this is used down the edge of the page
and throughout that neighbourhood section.

Prices
Multiple prices listed with reviews (eg €10/5 or
€10/5/20) indicate adult/child, adult/concession
or adult/child/family.

Send us your feedback We love to hear from
readers – your comments help make our books better. We read every word you send us, and we always
guarantee that your feedback goes straight to the
appropriate authors. The most useful submissions are
rewarded with a free book. To send us your updates
and find out about Lonely Planet events, newsletters
and travel news visit our award-winning website:
www.lonelyplanet.com/contact.

Note: We may edit, reproduce and incorporate your
comments in Lonely Planet products such as guidebooks, websites and digital products, so let us know
if you don't want your comments reproduced or your
name acknowledged. For a copy of our privacy policy
visit *www.lonelyplanet.com/privacy*.

ADAM SKOLNICK

Adam Skolnick was diagnosed with travel obses-
sion, for which there is no cure, while working as
an environmental activist in the mid-'90s and has
wandered six continents. A freelance journalist,
he writes about travel, culture, health, sports
and the environment for *Men's Health*, *Outside*,
Travel & Leisure and *Spa*. He has a soft spot for
Southeast Asia, a place that never fails to inspire
the beautiful and bizarre. On his Phuket research
trip he survived a brush with Thai mafia, an email
invasion from the romantically disgruntled, and
a motorcycle accident that left flesh wounds

and an ego bruise. He has co-authored three previous Lonely Planet
guidebooks, *Southeast Asia on a Shoestring*, *Mexico* and *East Timor*. You
can read more of his work at www.adamskolnick.com.

ADAM'S THANKS

Thanks to Jordan Whitley, Celine and Claude at Siam Indigo, John Grey,
Marco and Mam at Six Senses Hideaway, Dr Prasit, Khun Job, my friends
at German Bakery and Rum Jungle (that means you Tony, Jo, Kar and Jib),
the fabulous Wan at Sunrise Divers, to the keen eye of Austin Bush, and
to Carolyn Boicos and the Lonely Planet production team.

THE PHOTOGRAPHER

After working several years at a stable job, Austin Bush made the
questionable decision to pursue a career as a freelance photographer.
This choice has since taken him as far as Pakistan's Karakoram Hwy and
as near as Bangkok's Or Tor Kor Market. For samples of his work, check
www.austinbushphotography.com.

The diverse faces of Hat Karon (p68)

CONTENTS

Our authors are independent, dedicated travellers. They don't research using just the internet or phone, and they don't take freebies, so you can rely on their advice being well researched and impartial. They travel widely visiting thousands of places, taking great pride in getting all the details right and telling it how it is.

THIS IS PHUKET

Waking up with Phuket is glorious. Especially if you head to an out-of-the-way beach early enough to see the fishing boats return home. When the sun is just high enough to dance on the glassy Andaman Sea.

It's a scene that repeats itself up and down both coasts of this rather large tourist magnet. But it's the 17 west-coast beaches that lure 5.3 million tourists here annually. From the earthy, rocky coves on the south coast, to that wide web of lust that is pulsing Patong, to the gorgeous yet discreet north, Phuket's coastline contorts and twists into various shapes and sizes, giving each stretch of sand its own rhythm. But they all have one thing in common: their undeniable, soul-soothing beauty.

Phuket's rocky eastern shore is draped in thick mangroves and kissed by Ao Phang-Nga. With its luscious limestone islands guarding hidden lagoons fed by sea caves, and a network of underwater coral gardens where fluorescent schools of fish converge, this is Phuket's favourite aquatic playground.

The cultural heart is in Old Phuket, the stomping ground of the Baba people and a Sino-Portuguese treasure trove of mansions and shop houses, creaky teak shrines and local markets that unfurl alongside funky art galleries, hip restaurants, cafés and chic fashion boutiques. Elsewhere you can make offerings in Phuket's Buddhist temples and watch a white-robed flock stream into mosaic-domed mosques at sunset.

There's a lot to love about Phuket's appetite. With Thai curries and salads, a stunning selection of fresh seafood, upscale fusion kitchens and local roti and chicken stands, you have some eating to do. When the sun drops Phuket's wild side emerges. Think seedy go-go bars, stylish lounges, live rock and roll, and slick nightclubs hosting international DJs.

And if you stay up all night, you may find your way back to that quiet beach. Where you can watch the sunrise until it's high enough to dance once more.

Top Make an offering at Wat Phra Thong (p115) **Bottom** Relax in the shade of a beach umbrella on Hat Kamala (p96)

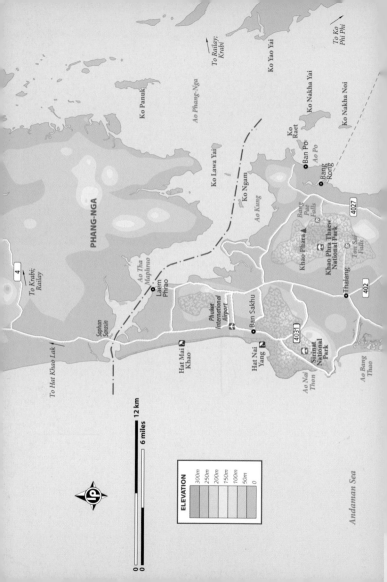

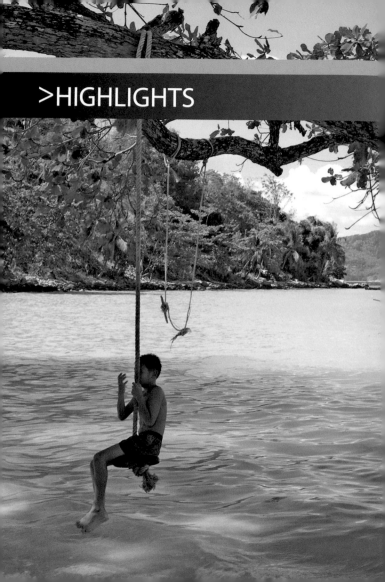

>HIGHLIGHTS

Get into the swing of things at Hat Tri-Triang (p54)

>1 KNEELING BEFORE BIG BUDDHA
VISITING PHUKET'S NEXT GREAT PILGRIMAGE SITE

Set on a hilltop just northwest of Chalong circle and visible from almost half of the island, Big Buddha (p74 and boxed text, p75) enjoys the best view in Phuket. To get here, follow the red signs from the main highway and wind up a country road, past terraced banana groves. Once you're on top, pay your respects at the tented golden shrine, then step up to Big Buddha's glorious plateau where you can peer into Kata's perfect bay, glimpse the shimmering Karon strand and, on the other side, survey the serene Chalong harbour, where the channel islands look like pebbles.

Of course, you'll be forgiven if you disregard the view for a few minutes to watch local craftsmen put the finishing touches on their 60-million baht Buddha, dressed in Burmese alabaster. When the sun hits him, he shines with enlightenment.

Over the past 20 years construction in Phuket hasn't stopped, so it means something when we call the Big Buddha Phuket's most important development project since the Sino-Portuguese buildings first went up over 100 years ago. Spearheaded by a local developer thirsty for good karma, more than 60 labourers and craftsmen have erected what at the time of publication was set to become one of the largest Buddha statues on earth. Initially, the statue was poured into a concrete mould laid horizontally. The figure was then cut into sections and a bamboo scaffold erected, so it could be reassembled vertically, like a spiritual jigsaw puzzle. Throughout construction fundraising efforts continued and thousands have contributed over 50 million baht (they need another 10 million) to see Big Buddha live.

The big guy definitely has an energetic pulse. As soon as you glimpse him from afar, he'll begin to pull you in, and once you have finally managed to get here, you'll want to linger for a while and enjoy the view, the silence, the wind and the rituals of the resident monks who stream around the property in saffron robes. And if you're really ambitious, you don't have to leave at all. Just check in to the free retreat centre, live with the monks and meditate in the big guy's holy shadow for as long as you like.

>2 IN THE FOOTSTEPS OF BABA
STROLLING THROUGH OLD PHUKET

Phuket's Old Town (p38) is about the narrow streets. There's sweet, romantic Soi Romanee, an alley with restored Sino-Portuguese relics, fabulous cafés and outdoor jazz concerts on the last Sunday of the month in the high season. Soi Soon Utis is another favourite, but few tourists roam this quiet residential street that ends at a canal. You should, because at the end of the road you'll find a box of almond cookies that might change your life. And no matter what, do not miss the Shrine of Serene Light (p43), the most ethereal and transporting of all the Chinese temples in the roughly 10 square blocks that comprise Phuket's enthralling Old Town.

There's something special about strolling through a town rich in history and culture, but if you stick to Phuket's tourist enclaves, where most of the Thai residents are from other parts of the country, you may never know that Phuket has a culture of its own. It developed more than 100 years ago when Chinese merchants and labourers sailed from southern China and landed here to work for European mining companies.

Over the next generation the Chinese and Thai intermarried, and their cultures fused. Their offspring became the first generation of Baba (local Phuket) people. They built large, airy and shady homes with European façades, and Chinese temples to honour their Taoist lineage, even while many were busy converting to Buddhism or Islam. Their food was likewise a mélange of southern Chinese and Thai tastes with sweet and smoky curries and an abundance of noodle dishes. And, of course, there are the Baba sweets – crafted from peanuts and cashews, almonds and coconuts, and dried fruit.

If you take the time to walk along Yaowari, Phang-Nga, Thalang, Rasada and Dibuk roads, diverting down all the little alleys you can find, you will discover all of the above. And you'll also come across countless art galleries, fashion boutiques, fusion restaurants, and charming bars and pubs that indicate this attractive town with a past also has one hell of a future.

>3 LOVE SONGS IN REHAB
HANGING WITH GIBBONS ON THEIR ROAD TO RECOVERY

As soon as you arrive you'll hear the gibbons' siren-like howls. But while their song is so obviously full of longing, it isn't freedom that moves them. It's love.

See, it's gibbon tradition that both males and females sing to find a mate. Think of it as Ape Idol meets Blind Date. Except here, at the Phuket Gibbon Rehabilitation Centre (p114), a project of the Wild Animal Rescue Foundation (WAR), the stakes are much higher. Solitary gibbons never make it out in the real, wild world. They will only successfully reintegrate if they have a family.

The biologists and volunteers who work here adopt these fluffy-faced, acrobatic white-handed gibbons, who were once kidnapped and forced to live as pets or as showpieces for street performers, and teach them how to behave like the gibbons they are.

Some were born into domesticity, but most were captured when they were babies, after they saw their parents killed. The statistics

don't lie. Each captive gibbon represents between two and three dead ones. The goal here is to slowly reintroduce them into the wild. You'll see them swinging in their large cages and singing to one another, because they know if they can lure a mate, they just might make it to freedom.

Consider Sam's story. Born in 1987, he was orphaned as a baby and lived in a Bangkok cage until he was three. That's when he was tied to the balcony railing of his owner's apartment. In 1994 his owner came home to find him wielding a knife in the kitchen. So, the man quickly called WAR. Unfortunately, Sam still won't sing. He never learned how. But most do, and so far there are three families of 13 gibbons living in the jungle above Bang Pae waterfall or on the man-made island WAR built in the nearby lake.

When they are ready to forage and live in holy matrimony, the gibbons are released into the forest. Once free, they swing from branch to branch at 25km per hour, eating fruit, nuts, insects and lizards. And they continue to sing – to one another, but also to other wild gibbons in the forest. It's a courtesy call, just to let them know that there's a new family in the neighbourhood.

>4 FRESH CATCH
TASTING RAWAI'S TANTALISING SEAFOOD

Wherever you go in Phuket you are never far from a local fish grill serving a mind-boggling selection of seafood just scooped from the Andaman Sea. But even given that context, Rawai is something special. Every day at around 3pm, the local fishermen, whose long-tail boats you may have seen twinkling along the horizon off the coast of Kata the night before, sort their catch at the village fish market, just to the left of the Rawai pier. That's when chefs, *faràng* and local, converge to pluck the best they can find. There will be red and white snapper, parrotfish, barracuda, rock lobster, crab – soft-shell, blue and red – mussels, sea snails, oysters and the most tender squid you can imagine.

Within an hour that same savoury selection is on ice in front of a strand of terrific local fish grills. Some have cushioned, candle-lit seating on the beachfront where the light bleeds pink at dusk. You can have your seafood steamed, fried and grilled, but make sure you forego that syrupy sweet and sour sauce – it came from a bottle. Ask for the fresh, vinegary, diced chilli sauce. It's spicy, but you can handle it. See p93 for more information.

>5 CAPE COVES
ENJOYING THE GREAT SOUTH-COAST BEACHES

Here's the key to Phuket bliss. Come to Hat Nai Han (pictured above; see p84) and stay for sunset. Wade into the warm sea, sheltered by two long, jungled, granite arms, play in the waves – or the tidal lagoon on the southern end if you have small children – look past the sailing yachts rising and falling with the swell and watch the sun burn a deep-orange streak in the sky. And that's just one moment on one of the superb beaches in the oft-ignored Rawai region.

Although millions of tourists descend on Patong, Kata and Karon, most never make the trek 10-minutes (by car) south to three outstanding beaches. Hat Nai Han is the most prominent, and arguably the most beautiful, but just north of it, accessed by a road that runs beneath the yacht club, is the wonderful Ao Sane beach (p86). With just one snack shack and a small stretch of boulder-strewn white sand, it's the sole domain of locals in the know. Further south, towards the Laem Phromthep lookout point, is Hat Ya Noi (p86). It's a bit rocky, which makes your entrance to the sea less than graceful, but it's also sheltered and rimmed with a rock reef that makes it ideal for snorkelling or paddling in a kayak, which you can hire on the sand. So take a day off from Kata's nubile sheen and commune with Mother Nature in the raw.

>6 HONG BY STARLIGHT

KAYAKING UNFORGETTABLE, LIMESTONE-STUDDED AO PHANG-NGA

Duck the midday hordes and slip through pitch-black bat caves into a hidden lagoon protected by massive limestone cliffs that rise spectacularly from the sea. You'll see monkeys, sea eagles, orchids and monitor lizards. Yes, this will be one fabulous kayaking trip (see p44 and boxed text, p122).

When iconoclastic American kayaker John Gray first encountered these *hongs* (caves semisubmerged in the sea) accessed through jagged caves at low tide, he knew he'd found something special, something he had to share. And he still feels that way. His Hong By Starlight evening tour promises solitude in hidden *hongs* that few locals know about. He'll explain how this fragile ecosystem is threatened and introduce you to the bay's famous translucence – a plankton-inspired light show that shines from the sea around the full moon. When Gray isn't on the water, he's banging the environmental gong and working to educate local students and the highest levels of the national park service. Of course, he's most in tune when he's on the water, because even while threatened, Ao Phang-Nga has innumerable natural gifts that are impossible to ignore. Especially if you're in a hull, carving another glassy lagoon as the sun drops.

>7 INTO THE WEE HOURS
TAKING THE OBLIGATORY, AND PROBABLY DEBAUCHEROUS, PATONG NIGHT TOUR

You've heard about the bar girls and go-go bars, the ladyboys (*kàthoey*; transvestites and transsexuals) and their drunken marks, but nothing quite prepares you for Th Bangla as the clock strikes midnight. Here you'll see dancing beauties in schoolgirl uniforms, and comely bar mavens who will take your cold hard cash by winning game after game of Connect Four (see boxed text, p66). Their power mystifies. You'll see street performers flaunting endangered species, some truly masterful magicians plying their trade for adoring crowds, and you will drink. You almost have to. But you don't have to stay on Th Bangla all night. With two new upscale clubs (see p66), Club Lime and Seduction, in full bloom, and nightly live music at Two Black Sheep (p66), Rock City (pictured above; p67) and Saxophone (p67), you have options that don't demand a moral compromise.

HIGHLIGHTS

>8 SUNSET SERENITY

EXPERIENCING DUSK AT LAEM PHROMTHEP

You won't be alone, but that won't matter once you scan the 270 degrees of Andaman Sea, noticing how elegantly it arcs around the cape below, where local fishermen cast into the waves from the jutting rocks.

OK, so you're not the type of traveller used to mingling with tour buses. We get it. But this time you'll make an exception. Because there's a reason the luxe buses line the road at the Laem Phromthep (p86) lookout point at around 6pm. With the possible exception of the Big Buddha, this is the best place to watch the sunset. Take it from the crowds, most of whom are Thai tourists. They spill onto the concrete platform, make offerings to the fantastic elephant shrine and climb to the top deck of the modern lighthouse shaped like a crab.

But if you really crave privacy, there's another option. Follow the handful of locals who walk down the fishermen's trail that hugs the ridge and ends on the rocks just a few metres above the sea. Although it looks like a thin strand from above, the peninsula – the island's true southernmost point – spreads out quite nicely, and you will easily find a nook of your own.

>9 THE ISLAND NEXT DOOR
DISCOVERING KO YAO NOI

Just an hour off the northeast coast of Phuket, and served by public boat, is one of Thailand's hidden gems, the laidback rural island of Ko Yao Noi (see p128). Nestled in the middle of Ao Phang-Nga and framed by soaring limestone karsts perfect for climbing, it's a relatively big island with steep rubber-treed mountains, seemingly endless white-sand beaches, and an infusion of warm energy from the ever-welcoming local people, over 90% of whom come from Muslim families who have lived here for generations.

A new five-star property, the Six Senses Hideaway Yao Noi (pictured above; see p129), a collection of thatched glass and wood villas with stunning views, opened here in late 2007. Its spa could be the best in the region. Paradise Hotel is another choice option if you just can't leave. And you should definitely stop by Pradu Seafood (p128), owned by Ya, a delightful local woman who has cooked for both Brad Pitt and Cameron Diaz. You'll sit under a thatched gazebo, across from a stilted fishing village, and dine on snapper steamed with lemongrass and garlic, or dry-rubbed with chilli and fried crispy brown. Yeah, you should probably stay the night.

>10 CLASS COOKING
LEARNING THAI CUISINE FROM THE MASTER

It's one thing to take a cooking class, it's another to learn at the ladle of Tummanoon Punchun, an award-winning executive chef at The Boathouse (p81) – long considered Phuket's finest kitchen. Punchun, who also travels to Europe to teach Thai cooking to renowned chefs in both Switzerland and Germany, has taught his weekend cooking classes to hotel guests for over a decade. Classes take place just off The Boathouse dining room, which has gorgeous views of Hat Kata. You'll be introduced to the herbs and spices that are the staple of any Thai kitchen, but you'll also learn how to use them without making the dish feel heavy. According to Punchun, who you may simply call, Chef, if you have the chemistry down, your curries will actually reduce fat and lower cholesterol. And you won't have to do the prep work. Chef's line cooks do the chopping. All you have to do is listen, learn and eat well. For details, see p77.

>PHUKET DIARY

Phuket needs no grand excuse to party. But locals are happy to have one. In addition to the festivals and events listed here, there are countless art openings, the occasional regatta gala and beach concert, and restaurants and clubs hosting special events that are open to the public. When national holidays do roll around, your experience may deepen. You can light candles on the beach during Loi Krathong, meditate at a temple then douse (and get doused by) strangers and friends on Songkran, and stare at a parade of the brutally pierced during Phuket City's singular Vegetarian Festival.

Songkran, a celebration of Thai Lunar New Year, is one big water fight (p26)

JANUARY & FEBRUARY

Chinese New Year

Ethnic Chinese residents in Phuket's Old Town decorate their homes, temples and streets with fruit, flowers and red banners during this two-day festival celebrating the Lunar New Year. Festivities include an elaborate dragon procession. Don't eat tofu this week. It's considered a bad omen. This celebration can occasionally occur in March.

Magha Puja

On the full moon of the third lunar month (usually during February) Buddhists stream into the island's temples to make offerings, pray and take part in candle-lit processions in commemoration of the day Lord Buddha first offered his teachings to over a thousand disciples at Veluwan Temple in India.

APRIL

Songkran

Water fight! Actually, it's a benevolent water war that celebrates the Thai Lunar New Year

Boys in costume, celebrating Chinese New Year

from 13 to 15 April. First, you go to temple to sprinkle water on Buddha images for good luck, then you take to the streets where you will be deluged with buckets and streams of water from all angles, also a harbinger of good luck. So, you may as well invest in a water gun and baptize others with some good fortune.

MAY

Visakha Puja

Observant Thais crowd the temples to hear sermons and pray on the May full moon, which doubles as the holiest day of the Buddhist calendar. It marks the birth, enlightenment and death of Buddha. There are candle lit processions in the evening, and this is also an ideal day to stockpile good karma by helping others.

JULY

Khao Phansa

Another lunar holiday, this one honours the beginning of Buddhist 'lent' in mid- to late July, when all monks are required to stay on temple grounds.

AUGUST

Por Tor Festival

The 'Hungry Ghosts' festival is an important event for ethnic Chinese in Phuket's Old Town. Special food, flowers and candles are presented to their ancestors' altars in order to feed the ghosts that have been released from hell for the month. You'll see plenty of vibrant cakes in the shape of turtles, which symbolise longevity. Worshippers believe their offerings will help ward off the reaper. Held 22 August to 3 September.

SEPTEMBER

Phuket Surfing Contest

www.phuketsurfingcontest.com
At the beginning of September Hat Kata swarms with surfers as the monsoon-fuelled swells reach their peak and parties ensue.

OCTOBER

Vegetarian Festival

www.phuketvegetarian.com
As much a spectacle as it is a festival, this cleansing ritual in Phuket's Old Town is marked by old men and women parading in trance and others who have pierced their cheeks, lips and tongues with sharp objects. And if you still have an appetite, there are lots of veggie goodies for sale on the streets. This festival can occur in late September.

Chulalongkorn Day

On the day of his death, 23 October, King Chulalongkorn is honoured for abolishing slavery and instituting widespread government reforms.

Taoist spirit medium in a trance, Vegetarian Festival (p27)

NOVEMBER

Loi Krathong

One of the most fun and accessible national holidays, crowds gather along Phuket's beaches under the full moon to honour the guardian spirit of water. Light a candle and some incense, place them on a banana leaf boat and send them out to sea.

DECEMBER

Phuket King's Cup Regatta

www.kingscup.com

Over 20 years old, this annual international yacht race means you'll probably stumble upon a boat party or three at Phuket's Yacht Haven.

New Year's Eve

Patong buzzes and thumps as gift, food and craft fairs invade the streets, live music is in the air and fireworks explode as the clock strikes midnight.

>ITINERARIES

Local transport at Hat Patong (p52)

ITINERARIES

Phuket is a large island, so it's best to explore it one bay (or neighbour-hood) at a time. Each region has plenty of activities and sights to keep you busy for several days, especially if you make time for swimming, lounging and a long lunch, which the sweltering heat will no doubt insist upon.

ONE DAY

Head into Phuket's Old Town early, so you can wander the narrow alleys before the sun sizzles. Stop by the Shrine of Serene Light (p43), grab a box of fresh almond cookies (see p46) on Soi Soon Utis and enjoy an or-ganic brunch at China Inn (p45). Pop into Wat Chalong (p88) on your way south, and spend the afternoon on Hat Nai Han (p84). Watch the sunset from Laem Phromthep (p86), then come back to Phuket's Old Town for dinner at Siam Indigo (p46) before hitting the Timber Hut (p49) and Ka Jok See (p48) for a little night music.

TWO DAYS

Arrange for a car and head to Thalang. Visit the Thalang National Mu-seum (p115) and Wat Phra Thong (p115) before entering the Khao Phra Thaew National Park (p114) and visiting the Phuket Gibbon Rehabilita-tion Centre (p114). Go to Bang Rong pier for a fresh seafood lunch (see p117), or skip that and head to one of the northern beaches. Choose Hat Surin (p101) if you want a bit of beach chic, and Hat Nai Yang (p121) if you're into an earthy scene. For dinner, fall into Ao Bang Thao's Tatonka (p110) for globe-trotter cuisine. Have a drink at The Catch Beach Club (p105) in Surin if you need a nightcap.

THREE DAYS

Spend the morning on beautiful Hat Kata Noi (p74). Have a late lunch at After Beach Bar (p82) just up the hill, then book time at The Sense Spa (p78) or the Spa Royale (p78). Take in the sunset at Big Buddha (p74) and come back to Hat Kata for dinner at The Boathouse (p81). Enjoy a late Happy Hour at JP's Restaurant & Bar (p65) in Patong, then dance like mad at Club Lime (p67).

Top left Devotee placing gold leaf on an image of a monk at Wat Chalong (p88) **Top right** The hustle and bustle of Hat Patong (p52) **Bottom** View over Hat Nai Han (p84)

RAINY DAY

If it's raining, hit the rainforest and visit the gibbons (p114) and waterfalls in Khao Phra Thaew National Park (p114). Then harness up for your Cable Jungle Adventure (p117). These zip lines are open rain or shine. Lunch at the Bang Rong pier (p117), where you can have grilled fish and contemplate the misty mangroves, then get clean at Sala Spa (p125) in Hat Mai Khao. Greet the dinner hour from The Ninth Floor (p64), where the rain will pound the floor-to-ceiling windows as Patong's lights glitter below.

FAMILY DAY

Begin the day with an hour-long elephant trek at Kok Chang Safari (p76) south of Kata. Continue on to Hat Nai Han (p84). Older kids will enjoy playing in the waves here (as long as it isn't monsoon season), and young children will feel comfortable in the shallow tidal lagoon. Grab some gelato at Arlecchino (p91) in Rawai, head to the Phuket Aquarium (p51)

Swoop along the zip lines at Cable Jungle Adventure (p117)

FORWARD PLANNING

Three weeks before you go If you haven't booked your room yet, you'd better. Phuket fills up in the high season, especially around Christmas, New Year's Eve and Chinese New Year. Check www.asia-hotels.com for last-minute hotel deals and availability. Phuket.com offers news on upcoming events, Jamie-monk.blogspot.com offers insider travel tips from a long-time local, and the *Bangkok Post* (www.bangkokpost.com) and the *Nation* (www.nationmultimedia.com) are both damn good and entertaining papers that detail the grit, glitz and politics of Thailand. And read the Thailand travel classic *The Beach* by Alex Garland.

One week before you go Book a seaside table at The Boathouse, and sign up for a dive course or dive trip. Once you have that sorted out, you can more easily schedule additional activities around your diving.

The day before you go Party all night so you'll snooze on the plane and wake up on Thai time. Oh, and stock up on sun block. It's expensive in Phuket.

to see the sharks, then it's onto the monkey platform in Ko Sireh (p50). On your way home stop for pizza and fruit shakes at The Cook (p47) in Phuket's Old Town.

ACTIVE DAY

Start with a morning dive or snorkel at Ko Waeo (p120). Then take a kite-boarding lesson (p123) on Hat Nai Yang. Grab lunch on the beach, then head to Hat Surin for a jet-ski ride (p102) and a parasail (p103), and if you're not exhausted yet, hit Rawai Muay Thai (p91) for an hour in the ring or bungy jump (p56) in Patong. Patrol the Patong Food Park (p63) for protein and Red Bull, then dance all night at Seduction (p67) or sit in with the band at Two Black Sheep (p66).

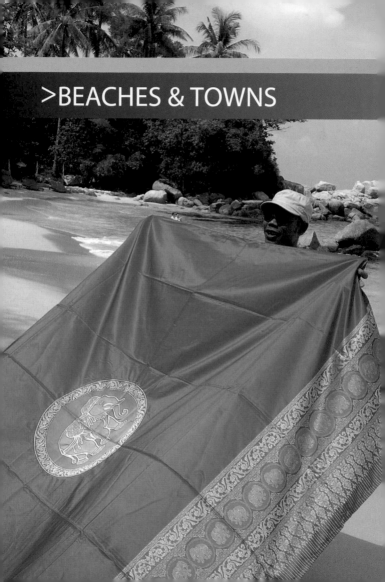

>BEACHES & TOWNS

Relax on Phuket's golden sands, and maybe buy a sarong

BEACHES & TOWNS

Your Phuket destiny will be predetermined. That's not to say free will plays no role in your tropical fate – it absolutely does. But due to Phuket's size there is really no feasible way to explore all of the luscious coves, funky markets and sweet sights in one journey. Which is why your holiday will be shaped by the address you have chosen long before your flight touches down.

The vast majority of visitors are attracted to the entrenched tourist magnets of Kata and Karon, and Patong. This is where you'll find a steady stream of sun-scorched Scandinavians who come for a social beach scene with, in Patong's case, thrumming nightlife. They are also centrally located, so it's possible to get from here to Phuket City and Laem Phromthep in 30 minutes or less.

Hat Surin, north of Patong, is quintessential barefoot elegance. The cove is gorgeous, compact and intimate, and its beachfront dining scene is unparalleled on the island. Prices are high in Surin, but that's the way upscale postcodes work.

South of Surin, Kamala has a Jimmy Buffet vibe. It gets a midlife crisis spill-over from Patong (one bay down), but the affordable lodging and beachfront walk attract young families, too. Further north, Ao Bang Thao is the island's current investment vortex. Villas, hotels and restaurants are replicating across marshland on the outskirts of traditional fishing villages.

Phuket's poles are tantalising. The far north is home to Phuket's secluded white sand, and some exceptional resorts, within a short boat ride of terrific snorkelling and diving. Rawai, perched at the southernmost tip, has some of Phuket's best beaches, fantastic food and an engaging local community that dates back generations.

And don't even consider ignoring Phuket's Old Town. If the historic architecture and local Baba culture don't captivate you, the fabulous shopping, dining and nightlife will.

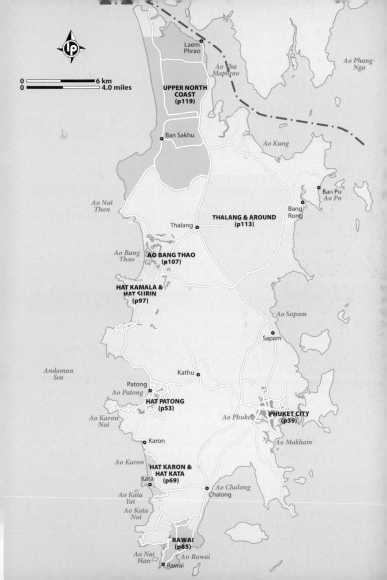

Laem
Phrao

Ao Tha
Maphrao

Ao Phang-
Nga

**UPPER NORTH
COAST**
(p119)

Ban Sakhu

Ao Kung

Ao Nai
Thon

Ban Po
Ao Po

Bang
Rong

Thalang

THALANG & AROUND
(p113)

Bang
Rong

Ao Bang
Thao

AO BANG THAO
(p107)

**HAT KAMALA &
HAT SURIN**
(p97)

Ao Sapam

Sapam

*Andaman
Sea*

Kathu

Patong
Ao Patong

HAT PATONG
(p53)

Ao Phuket

PHUKET CITY
(p39)

Ao Karon
Noi

Ao Makham

Karon

Ao Karon

**HAT KARON &
HAT KATA**
(p69)

Kata

Ao Chalong

Chalong

Ao Kata
Yai

Ao Kata
Noi

RAWAI
(p85)

Ao Nai
Han

Ao Rawai

Rawai

>PHUKET CITY & AROUND

One of the least visited, and most authentic corners of the island, Phuket City (aka Phuket Town) is a magical place to wander. Here you'll find eclectic art galleries, fantastic shopping, crumbling Sino-Portuguese relics, Chinese Taoist shrines, the island's best nightclubs and some damn good food.

True story. Phuket was once dominated by an industry other than tourism – tin mining. The southern Chinese immigrants who first arrived in Phuket in the 19th century to work the tin mines lived among these narrow alleys and canals. Within a generation Phuket had its own subculture. Lifelong Phuket City residents celebrate their Chinese heritage through both ritual and cuisine, and yet the town – especially the architecture – has a distinctly European vibe.

But it's not just some lost-in-time cultural archive. Bubbling up throughout the emerging Old Town (see p14) is an infusion of relevant art and music, and an abundance of hip restaurants and cafés. It's no wonder that people who live and work in Phuket spend their evenings here.

PHUKET CITY & AROUND

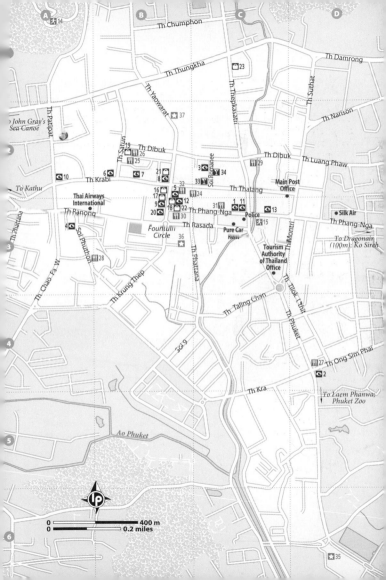

👁 SEE

👁 ART HOME

☎ 076 224866; amnat_boonsanit@
yahoo.com; 113 Th Phang-Nga;
admission free; ⏰ 10am-7pm

They certainly sound basic
(canvases of leaves, pots, fish and
spheres), but they come with a
unique Zen, modernist twist.

👁 BANG NIEW SHRINE

Th Ong Sim Phai; admission free;
⏰ 6am-6pm

Built in 1934, this shrine honours
Lao La as principal deity and hosts
local Chinese opera productions.

👁 BOBOL'S ART GALLERY

Soi Romanee; admission free;
⏰ 10am-6pm

VEGETARIAN FESTIVAL

The Vegetarian Festival, Phuket's most important festival, takes place during the first nine
days of the ninth lunar month of the Chinese calendar – usually late September or October.

It celebrates the beginning of the month of 'Taoist Lent', when devout Chinese abstain
from eating meat. In Phuket, the festival activities are centred around five Chinese temples
and shrines, with the Jui Tui Tao Bo Keng (opposite) on Soi Puthon the most important, followed by Bang New (above) and Sui Boon Tong shrines. Events are also celebrated at temples
in the nearby towns of Kathu (where the festival originated) and Ban Tha Reua.

Besides abstention from meat, the Vegetarian Festival involves various processions culmi-
nating with incredible acts of self-mortification – walking on hot coals, piercing the skin with
sharp objects and so on. Shop owners along Phuket's central streets set up altars in front of
their shopfronts offering nine tiny cups of tea, incense, fruit, candles and flowers to the nine
emperor gods invoked by the festival. Those participating as mediums bring the nine deities
to earth for the festival by entering into a trance state and piercing their cheeks with all
manner of objects – sharpened tree branches, spears, slide trombones; some even hack their
tongues continuously with saw or axe blades – this is the hardest to watch. During the street
processions these mediums stop at the shopfront altars, where they pick up the offered fruit
and either add it to the objects piercing their cheeks or pass it on to bystanders as a blessing.
They also drink one of the nine cups of tea and grab some flowers to stick in their waistbands.
The shop owners and their families stand by with their hands together in a *wâi* gesture, out
of respect for the mediums that are temporarily possessed by the deities.

The entire atmosphere is one of religious frenzy, with deafening firecrackers, ritual dancing
and bloodstained shirts. Oddly there is no record of this kind of activity associated with Taoist Lent
in China. The local Chinese claim that the festival was started by a theatre troupe from China that
stopped off in nearby Kathu around 150 years ago. The story goes that the troupe was struck seri-
ously ill because the members had failed to propitiate the nine emperor gods of Taoism. The nine-
day penance they performed included self-piercing, meditation and a strict vegetarian diet.

For more info, visit www.phuketvegetar.com.

Bobol, a reclusive French artist who has lived above the gallery for nearly 20 years, paints colourful canvases with Asian and Indian influences. Leaf through his fraying sketchbook.

JUI TUI TAO BO KENG SHRINE

Soi Puthon; admission free; ⏱ **6am-6pm**
This shrine attracts those wishing to bolster their physical health through prayer. It's also a base for serious (read: violently pierced) participants during the Vegetarian Festival (see boxed text, opposite), which makes it a great place to stake out and snap photos like the cultural paparazzi.

NUMBER 1 GALLERY

☎ **087 2815279; www.number1gallery .com; 32 Th Yaowarat; admission free;** ⏱ **10.30am-7.30pm**
Modern interpretations of traditional themes can be found at the Phuket branch of one of Bangkok's best loved fine-art galleries. Gold leaf and acrylic formed evocative images of blooming lotuses and Asian elephants when we visited.

PHRA PHITAK CHYN PRACHA MANSION

9 Th Krabi; admission free
The namesake of this now abandoned, ochre-tinted mansion once owned a number of tin mines in the early 20th century. The mansion now sits forlorn, in need of a Thai Scarlett O'Hara (it certainly has the grounds for it). The iron gates are open, so proceed at your own risk. If you do breach the threshold, and dogs bark, don't worry they're probably just growling at the ghosts.

PHUKET THAI HUA MUSEUM

www.thaihua.net; Th Krabi; admission free; ⏱ **1-8pm Tue-Sun**
This new museum set in an old Sino-Portuguese home celebrates the town's Chinese heritage. It consists mostly of old and new black-and-white photographs and runs on donations.

Unloading outside Phuket Thai Hua Museum

Dr Prasit Koysiripong
Chairman of the Old Phuket Foundation

What inspired you to lead the renovation of Phuket's Old Town? I don't want to see my culture disappear. **So this isn't a strategy to lure tourists?** Yes, we hope this becomes a heritage destination, but not just for international tourists, for Thai people and for Phuket people. **What are your current plans?** We are repainting the local homes free of charge. We are also removing the wires from in front of the façades and hiding them. We also sponsor a jazz concert on Soi Romanee on the last Sunday of every month, and we hope to sponsor a weekend market there very soon. **What does the future hold for Phuket's Old Town?** We feel this will be an international city, and when people come we will be able to give them a connection to Phuket's past so they can become Phuketian, too.

RENDEZVOUS GALLERY
☎ 076 219095; 69 Th Yaowarat; admission free; ⏱ 10am-7pm
Fantastic psychedelic Buddhist art on canvas, batik, paper and wood.

RINDA MAGICAL ART
☎ 089 2898852; www.rindamagicalart.com; 27 Th Yaowarat; admission free; ⏱ 10am-7pm
Want to smile? Step inside this swirling mélange of whimsical surrealism. The 30-something owner artists are a joy to chat with. They give art classes on the premises (but only take serious students) and they also teach art in Phuket's juvenile detention facility.

SAM SAN SHRINE
Th Krabi; admission free; ⏱ 6am-6pm
This Taoist Chinese shrine isn't long on history, but the incense plumes and warbling lyre should provide a head change for Lao Tzu lovers.

SARASIL ART GALLERY
☎ 081 0832873; somkiatkaewnok@yahoo.com; 121 Th Phang-Nga; admission free; ⏱ 10am-7pm
Sarasil's mixed media canvases seem influenced by the magical realism of Mexico, Africa and his native Thailand.

SHRINE OF SERENE LIGHT
Saan Jao Sang Tham; admission free; ⏱ 8.30am-noon & 1.30-5.30pm

Built by a local family in 1889, but tucked away behind Wilai restaurant and accessible via a narrow walk marked by a red arch off Th Phang-Nga, is the Old Town's most striking Chinese shrine. You'll see Taoist etchings on the walls, the vaulted ceiling is stained from incense plumes. The altar is always alive with fresh flowers and burning candles.

SIAM ART GALLERY
☎ 087 899212; siamart95@gmail.com; 95 Th Phang-Nga; admission free; ⏱ 10am-7pm
Striking work that is feminine, big-eyed innocent and slightly off kilter.

DO
KHAO RANG
Sightseeing
Rang Hill
Savour the spectacular views of the city from this public park situated northwest of the town centre. You can drive up the paved road, although if you want the exercise you can walk. It's a nice workout, even if you have to dodge the snarling mob of dogs. (You've heard the expression about barks and bites. It applies here.) The shade and the view will make it hard to leave once you've arrived.

BEACHES & TOWNS

PHUKET CITY & AROUND

🏄 JOHN GRAY'S SEA CANOE
Watersports

☎ 076 254505; www.johngray-sea canoe.com; 124 Soi 1, Th Yaowarat; trips from 3950B

Located west of town, Phuket's original kayak outfitter, John Gray, and his team of local guides lead ecotours to Ao Phang-Nga's hidden islands, lagoons and *hongs* (caves semisubmerged in the sea), where guests learn about this fragile eco-system. His guided evening paddle through bat caves into biolumi-nescent lagoons, is unforgettable. Overnight camping trips are also available. For more information, see p20 and boxed text, p122.

🏃 PHUKET ZOO
Animal Interaction

☎ 076 381227; www.phuketzoo.com; 23/2 Moo 3 Soi, Th Phalai Chaofa; admission 200B; 🕗 8.30am-6pm

Young animal lovers will enjoy the monkey, elephant and crocodile shows, as well as the butterfly farm.

🏄 SEALAND ADVENTURE
CAMP *Adventure, Sports*

☎ 076 222900; 125/1 Th Phang-Nga; trips per day from 1500B

This Phuket City–based outfitter can put you on the back of an elephant or a mountain bike. Or if you prefer, it can put you in a 4WD, or immerse you in a nearby jungle or river.

🛍 SHOP
🛍 BAN BORAN TEXTILES
Fashion

☎ 076 211563; 51 Th Yaowarat; 🕗 10am-7pm

Simply put, this dusty hole in the wall is the best shop on the island for silk, raw silk, and cotton textiles and sarongs.

🛍 CHÁCO *Fashion*
☎ 076 216213; 41 Th Yaowarat; 🕗 10am-8pm

A flash boutique that looks like it was shipped straight from Rodeo Drive. The designs range from trendy to classic and it produces custom suits, shirts and dresses.

🛍 DOWNTOWN PLAZA
MARKET *Market*

South of Th Thalang; 🕗 8am-3pm

Ramshackle stalls with a host of fruit, vegetables, fish, chicken, sweets and spices. Comes com-plete with all requisite market aromas, from sweet to funky.

🛍 ISLAND PARADISE *Fashion*
🕗 076 256418; 8 Th Phang-Nga; 🕗 10am-9pm

Set in the same old relic as Siam Indigo, this lovely and expansive hippie-chic boutique, featuring nothing but up-and-coming Thai designers, has stylishly flowing dresses, silk skirts and blouses, and exceptional jewellery. This shop is a must.

🔲 LILAC *Fashion*
☎ 076 226187; 19 Th Yaowarat;
🕑 9am-6pm
Lilac is further proof that Phuket's best shopping is in Phuket City. Everything – the velvet pillows, silk scarves, blouses and skirts, cute handbags and fantastic sandals – is handmade.

🔲 ORIENTAL ORIGIN *Fashion*
97 Th Dibuk; 🕑 10am-7pm Mon-Sat
This old wooden house and lovely garden courtyard are filled with the traditional art, jewellery, antiques and clothes of old Phuket.

🔲 RED DOOR GALLERY
Design, Homewares
☎ 076 270833; 17 Yaowarat Rd;
🕑 9am-5pm
A relatively spare yet sophisticated gallery that has both antique and new production Southeast Asian art.

🔲 SHARMS
Design, Jewellery
☎ 076 218514; 83/85 Th Yaowarat;
🕑 10am-7pm
Moroccan art and gifts can be found here, along with a cool collection of antique glass, some sensational jewellery and a smattering of Art Deco furniture.

🔲 SOUTHWIND BOOKS *Books*
☎ 089 7242136; 1/3/5 Th Phang-Nga;
🕑 9am-7pm Mon-Sat, 10am-3pm Sun
Bookworms will love perusing the dusty stacks at this second-hand bookshop. It has titles in 18 languages, including Polish. You might stumble onto a forgotten first edition.

🔲 V MULTI-GEMS *Jewellery*
☎ 076 212715; 154 Thepkrasatri Rd;
🕑 9am-6pm Mon-Sat
Peruse cases of rubies, pearls and sapphires. Sure it also has hideous print shirts for him and cheesy tea sets for her, but check out those strands of light-bending cultured pearls. Great deals abound.

🍴 EAT

🍴 CHINA INN *Thai* $$
☎ 076 356239; 20 Th Thalang;
🕑 9am-6pm Mon-Thu, 9am-10pm Fri & Sat; Ⓥ ⓑ
The organic movement meets traditional Phuket cuisine at this renovated turn-of-the-century shophouse. As well as home-made yoghurt and fruit smoothies flavoured with organic honey, there's are many vegetarian options, including a *massaman* curry (a thick curry of chicken, beef or pork stewed in potatoes and usually peanuts) with tofu, and a favourite Phuket dish, red curry with crab.

BEACHES & TOWNS

PHUKET CITY & AROUND

🍴 COOKIE HOUSE

Bakery $

☎ 076 258050; Soi Soon Utis; ⚐

There's no sign, but Mi Han, the young matriarch of this old Sino-Portuguese house located at the dead end of tranquil Soi Soon Utis, does make some fabulous cookies from freshly pulverised almond paste, egg yolks and butter. Consider them a flaky and sweet, but not too sweet, Phuket delicacy.

🍴 DIBUK RESTAURANT

French, Thai $$$

☎ 076 258148; 69 Th Dibuk; ⚐ 11am-midnight

More a marriage of French and Thai than actual fusion, you can have your duck paté and wild boar in red-wine sauce, or steamed whole snapper and searing hot prawns steeped in mint, lemongrass and lime juice. Whichever nation you choose, the food works and considering the quality, the price is quite reasonable.

🍴 LA GAETANA

Italian $$$

☎ 076 250523; 352 Th Phuket; ⚐ noon-2pm & 6-10pm Thu-Tue; Ⓥ

An irresistibly intimate five-table restaurant, La Gaetana has black-concrete floors, colourful walls and stemware, an open kitchen in the courtyard and a superb Italian menu. Treat yourself to the duck breast *carpaccio* followed by the osso bucco.

🍴 NATURAL RESTAURANT

Thai $$

☎ 076 224287; www.naturalrestaurant -phuket.com; 62/5 Soi Puthon; ⚐ 10.30am-11.30pm; ⚐

A Phuket City staple for 15 years, this is a good place for traditional Thai food. The eclectic ambiance is a treat.

🍴 SHINTARO

Japanese $$

85 Th Dibuk; ⚐ 6pm-midnight

This mod bento box of a restaurant offers good sushi, *shabu shabu* and *yakitori*. Eat under the stars or in private white-vinyl dining cubes – they're huge booths with sliding doors.

🍴 SIAM INDIGO

Fusion $$$

☎ 076 256697; www.siamindigo.com; 8 Th Phang-Nga; ⚐ 5pm-late Mon-Sat

A stylish, whitewashed, shabby-chic gem, nestled in an 80-year-old Sino-Portuguese relic that specialises in Royal Thai cuisine with a twist. There's a fiery seared tuna *larb* (minced chicken, beef or pork salad mixed with chilli, mint and coriander), minced and spiced pork satay roasted on steamed

Local art, local food at Siam Indigo

lemongrass, grilled duck breast sliced and stewed in a *massaman* curry, as well as a few Phuketian dishes, including *gaeng poo*, a sweet and spicy crab-meat curry. Siam Indigo has style, soul (check out the work of local artists on the walls) and insane food, which makes it one of the best restaurants on the island, if not the best. Don't miss it.

🍴 THE COOK
Thai, Italian $
☎ 076 258375; 101 Th Phang-Nga;
🕐 11am-10pm; Ⓥ 🚸

The Thai chef used to cook Italian at a megaresort, so when he opened this ludicrously inexpensive Old Town café he fused the two. Which is why you'll order the sensational green curry pizza with chicken or the pork curry coconut milk pizza and love it. Thank god for globalisation.

🍴 WILAI
Thai $
☎ 076 222875; 14 Th Thalang;
🕐 7am-2pm; 🚹 🚸

Local Phuket food is fried and steamed at this local lunch counter. Its speciality is noodles. It does a Phuketian *pàt tai* (Thai fried noodles, usually with peanuts) that has some kick to it, and a fantastic seafood *mee sua*. Think: noodles sautéed with egg, greens, prawns, chunks of sea bass and incredibly tender squid. Wash it down with fresh chrysanthemum juice. We call it Phuket soul food.

🍸 DRINK
🍸 BO(OK)HEMIAN
Café
☎ 076 258254; 61 Th Thalang;
🕐 9am-10pm; 🖳

Every town should have a coffee house this cool. The split-level open design feels both warm and leading edge. They have wi-fi, used DVDs and books to buy and borrow, gourmet coffee and tea, and an outrageously delicious chocolate cake.

▼ GLASTNÖST
Café

☎ 084 0580288; 14 Soi Romanee

There is nothing better on a relentless Phuket City afternoon than to slip into this café that doubles as a law office and sip iced Ceylon tea or traditional Phuket coffee brewed by the lawyer himself, while jazz blares on the sound system. Sometimes the jazz is live – if the resident Bossa Nova man is in town. Call three hours ahead and you can have a traditional Phuket meal for four (2000B), cooked by the man who represents Greenpeace in Thailand.

▼ ROCKIN' ANGELS
Bar

☎ 089 6549654; www.rockinangels .com; 54 Th Yaowarat; ⏰ 5pm-1am

This small but colourful Old Town bar is decorated with framed singles and LPs – Peter Frampton, Stevie Wonder, Van Halen, Survivor, Oasis and the Village People are all represented (yes, the Village People may have invented phone sex). Weekend nights can get wild when Patrick, the Singaporean-born owner, jams with his house band and whoever wants to sit in. The beers are cold, the drinks are cheap, and the crowd composed of Thai and expat locals.

▼ TEA HOUSE
Café

☎ 089 6549654; 55 Th Yaowarat; ⏰ 3pm-12.30am

A homage to the tea times of Phuket City's Chinese past, this is the only place where you'll enjoy tea from a traditional clay pot. It has nine varieties, including oolong, white, green and chrysanthemum, and staff will refill the pot until you say 'when'.

★ PLAY

★ BOXING STADIUM
Stadium

South of Phuket City, near the pier; admission general/ringside incl one-way transport 1300/1500B; ⏰ from 8pm Tue & Fri

Muay thai (Thai boxing) can be witnessed here twice a week. Ticket prices vary depending on where you sit and include one-way transport. Get your tickets at the OnOn Hotel on Th Phang-Nga.

★ KA JOK SEE
Club

☎ 076 217903; 26 Th Takua Pa; admission free; ⏰ 6pm-1am Tue-Sun

Ostensibly, this is a restaurant, and, by all accounts, a quite good one. But it has two identities, and once the tables are cleared it becomes a bohemian madhouse

Calories on, calories off – eat at Ka Jok See, then boogie into the small hours

and the kind of party you've always wanted to go to. The superb music bounces between soul, rare groove, ambient and hip-hop. Some folks get on the mic, others bang away on bongos and everyone must dance.

⭐ TIMBER HUT
Club

☎ 076 211839; 118/1 Th Yaowarat; admission free; ⏰ 6pm-2am

Thai and expat locals have been filling this big, old wooden clubhouse every night for 18 years. They gather at the wooden tables on two floors, converge around thick timber columns, swill whiskey and sway to live bands that swing from hard rock to funk to hip-hop with aplomb. Unlike many of the island's nightclubs, this place has soul to spare.

BEACHES & TOWNS

PHUKET CITY & AROUND

KO SIREH

This tiny island, 4km east of the capital and connected to the main island by a bridge, is known for its *chao leh* (sea gypsy) village (Map pp8–9), ravenous monkeys and a massive hilltop reclining Buddha. It receives few tourists, so it's a nice place to visit if you want a dose of the local vibe. On the eastern side of the island is a public beach called Hat Teum Suk, with a few chairs and thatched-roof shelters. The beach isn't gorgeous but the views are lovely.

👁 SEE

👁 WAT SIREH
Th Sireh; admission free
Perched on Sireh's highest point, and accessed by a driveway adjacent to the school, is an overgrown, sun-faded temple surrounded by dozens of gold-painted Buddhas. Inside is a massive reclining Buddha, and the verandas offer even more impressive 270-degree sea views.

🏃 DO

🏃 FEED THE MONKEYS
Animal Interaction
Monkey Platform near the bridge; admission free
Just after crossing over onto the island you'll see a wooden platform with monkey carvings overlooking the mangroves. Inside those mangroves are hundreds of Macaque monkeys, and at sunset locals feed them from the platform. It is quite a scene – chaotic and exhilarating.

🏃 PHUKET THAI COOKERY SCHOOL *Cooking Class*
☎ 076 252354; www.phuket-thai cookeryschool.com; 39/4 Thepatan Rd; per day 1900B; ⏰ 8.30am-10.30pm
Set on a quiet seafront plot on the east coast is a popular cooking school. Courses begin twice daily at 10am and 3pm, and include hotel pick-ups, market tours and a cookbook.

LAEM PHANWA

Laem Phanwa (Map pp8–9) is a slender cape, jutting into the sea on the southeastern coast of Phuket. It's a very mellow corner of the island that is infused with local culture. Because it's not well served by roads to Phuket's tourist beaches, most international visitors and residents ignore it. You shouldn't. Beauty and authenticity are everywhere. To get to the cape, take Hwy 4021 and then turn south down Hwy 4023 just outside Phuket City.

Phuket Aquarium is the best place for fish to get an up-close look at humans

SEE
PHUKET AQUARIUM
☎ 076 391126; adult/child 100/50B;
⏰ 8.30am-4pm

Located at the tip of the cape, the 32 tanks display a varied collection of tropical fish and other marine life. Stroll through the tunnel to glimpse life beneath the surface.

🍴 EAT
SEAFOOD STALLS
Seafood $

Laem Phanwa waterfront; admission free; ⏰ 11am-11pm

A great place to devour fresh seafood and watch the painted fishing boats and long tails bob by.

>HAT PATONG

With its complete disregard for managed development and its penchant for turning the midlife crisis into a full-scale industry, Patong is rampant with unintentional comedy. But take one look at the wide white-sand beach and magnificent crescent bay, and you'll understand how all this started.

Patong has its charms. Along with numerous diving and spa options, there's upscale dining, campy cabaret, *muay thai* (Thai boxing), dusty antique shops and street-side fish grills. The pristine beaches to the south are soul soothing, and if you crave a quiet patch on Hat Patong, you can head to the more serene northern end. In fact, after a few days, even haters start to enjoy it. That's when its time to leave, or your standards and sense of humour will suffer.

HAT PATONG

⊙ SEE

Good Luck Shrine	1	B1
J&L Motorbike Shop	2	C3
Mae Ubol Market	3	C5
Wat Suwankhiri	4	D2

🏃 DO

All 4 Diving	5	B3
Amala Spa	6	C2
Big Bike Company	(see 2)	
First Foot Relax 2	7	B4
Let's Relax	8	B5
Nicky's Handlebar	9	C2
Ocean Bowl Phuket	10	B4
Ocean Divers	11	B3
Paraphat Sea Sports Club	12	B4
Pum Cooking School	13	B5
Scandinavian Divers	14	B4
Scuba Cat	15	A5
Sunrise Diving	16	B3
Swasana Spa	17	B3
Wang Sauna	18	C6
Warm Water Divers	19	B5
Water World Asia	20	B5

🛍 SHOP

Amarit	21	C3
Baan Thai Antiques	22	A5
Baanboonpitak	23	A6
Banzaan Shopping Plaza	24	C5
Jung Ceylon	25	B4
Mango Tree	26	A6
Mitsuko	27	B4
Siam Ceramic	28	A5
The Royal King Collection	29	A5

🍴 EAT

3 Spices	(see 17)	
Ali Baba	30	A5
Baan Rim Pa	31	B1
Cocoa Nut	32	B4
Dang Restaurant	33	B4
Floyd's Brasserie	34	A5
Fried Chicken	35	C1
Hot Curry	36	B5
Hung Fat's	37	B1
Mengrai Seafood	38	B4
Newspaper	39	C4
Patong Food Park	40	C3
Sala Bua	(see 17)	
Savoey	41	B4
Takumi	42	B3
Tantra	43	B3
The Ninth Floor	44	B5
The Orchids	45	A5
Yean Korean BBQ	46	B5

🍸 DRINK

I'm Caffé	47	C5
JP's Restaurant & Bar	(see 6)	
Monte's	48	C3
Two Black Sheep	49	B4

★ PLAY

Bangla Boxing Stadium	50	B4
Club Lime	51	B3
Rock City	(see 51)	
Saxophone	(see 51)	
Seduction	52	B4

A
B
C
D

To Hat Kalim;
Hat Kamala; Lim's
🍴 37
🍴 31
1
📷 1
🍴 35
Th Phra Barami
📷 4
2
To Kathu;
Jungle Bungy Jump
Th Chaloem Phra Kiat
Th Kalim Beach
● Post Office
🚶 6
🍴 9
🍴 40
🍴 44
Th Hat Patong
Th Rat Uthit
Th Pisit Karani
3
★ 51
🍴 43
Ao Patong
16 🚶
42 📷
17 🚶
Th Trawiwong
🚶 5
Th Sawatdirak
📷 21
🍴 11
📷 2
48 🍸
Hat Patong
🍴 39
32 🍴
33 🍴
🍴 12
49 🍸
4
Tourist Police ●
🍴 41
27 📷
Th Bangla
10 🚶
🍴 38
🚶 52
7 🚶
14 🍴
50 📷
Soi Saen
Sabai
25 📷
📷 24
Th Na Nai
Post Office
15 🚶 ●
22 🍴
45 🍴
13 🚶
🚶 20
36 🍴
8 🍴
46 🍴
28 📷
29 📷
5
Soi Kepsap
🚶 19
47 🍸
3 📷
To Freedom Beach;
Hat-Tri-Triang; Jet Ski Patong Bay;
Long-tail Charters; La Grita; Breeze Bar
30 📷
34 🍴
Th Ruamchai
18 🚶
6
Th Prachanukhro
23 📷
📷 26
To Hat Karon; Hat Kata;
Arawan Bukit Elephant Trekking;
Simon Cabaret

0   500 m
0   0.3 miles

👁 SEE

👁 FREEDOM BEACH

Accessible by long-tail boat from Hat Patong; return boat trips 1500B
Just 15 minutes away, but a whole different world. If Patong is suffocating you, then you will find freedom on this pristine slice of golden sand.

👁 GOOD LUCK SHRINE

cnr Th Kalim Beach & Th Phra Barami; admission free
A lovely, golden Bodhisattva statue, guarded by carved elephants festooned with flowers, incense and candles, with a sea backdrop. This is a nice spot to connect with the divine or simply make a wish and savour the sound of... silence.

👁 HAT TRI-TRIANG

Th Thawiwong; admission free
Can you really find peace on a beach just around the corner from Patong? Hell yes. Sheltered by boulders to the north and a headland to the south, this tiny bay is an antidote for your Patong-weary soul. You won't even see the sprawl.

👁 J&L MOTORBIKE SHOP

106 Th Rat Uthit; admission free
It looks like an ordinary garage, but inside are some amazing demonic dinosaur sculptures crafted from old motorcycle parts. A must see for all 10-year-olds.

👁 MAE UBOL MARKET

Th Na Nai; admission free; ⏱ 7am-noon & 5pm-4am
This market has two shifts. In the morning, head to the warehouse, where you can see a bustling fresh market hard at haggle. It's an entertaining scene. At 5pm the night market opens for business, meaning you can eat good Thai food and fresh seafood all night long if you want to.

👁 WAT SUWANKHIRI

Th Phisit Karani; admission free
Unlike some of the more tourist-friendly temples, this overgrown compound sports rambling roosters, sleeping dogs and (usually) locked temple doors. But the tiered roof of the cremation shrine is lovely, and the warbling voice of a monk reciting scripture over the PA lends the scene some poetry.

🏃 DO

🏃 ALL 4 DIVING *Watersports*

☎ 076 344611; www.all4diving.com; 5/4 Th Sawatdirak; day trips from 2900B; ⏱ 9am-9pm
Not just a full-service dive school (staff can teach you to become a dive master if you have the

required 55 logged dives) and recreational dive centre, but also one of the best dive superstores in Phuket. It also books live aboards to the Similan Islands and day trips to local reefs (Ko Racha Yai and Sharkpoint, among them).

AMALA SPA *Spa*
☎ 076 343024; www.bydlofts.com; 5/28 Th Rat Uthit; treatments from 600B; ☺ 9am-8pm
Like the rest of the BYD property, this spa offers luxurious urban design, as well as Thai, oil and reflexology massage, a white-clay body wrap or a detoxifying green-tea body polish.

ARAWAN BUKIT ELEPHANT TREKKING *Animal Interaction*
☎ 086 8094780; Th Patong-Karon; tours 400-1200B; ☺ 9am-6pm
Peter, Gulong and their pachyderm mates are logging industry refugees. They sleep five hours a day, eat six hours a day and will carry you to commanding views of Ao Patong.

BIG BIKE COMPANY *Adventure, Sports*
☎ 076 345100; www.bigbikecompany .com; 106 Th Rat Uthit; hire per day 900B; ☺ 9am-6pm
Envision something bigger between your legs? Ditch the

Hire a powerful ride at the Big Bike Company

wimpy motor scooter and hop onto one of these Honda CB 400cc machines. The highway (especially that winding stretch of road north of Patong) awaits.

FIRST FOOT RELAX 2 *Spa*
☎ 076 340248; 54/7 Soi Patong Resort; massage from 450B; ⏱ 9am-midnight
Although pricier than most shop-front massage joints, First Foot Relax 2 is worth it – in fact, it's in a league of its own. There are mosaic washbowls for reflexology clients, the dark-wood interior is infused with lemongrass, and baskets bloom with fresh towels. Splurge and get the seaweed and mud wrap before your massage.

JET SKI PATONG BAY
Watersports
Nong Kwan Marine Rentals; Southern entrance to Th Thawiwong; per hr 3000B
If you can't ignore 'em, join 'em. You'll get a buzz, but may lose your hearing, so wear the ear-plugs. There are similar outfitters scattered along the beach. They all charge the same price.

JUNGLE BUNGY JUMP
Extreme Sports
☎ 076 321351; www.phuket.com /bungy; 61/3 Moo 6, Kathu; single jump 1600B
In operation since 1992, this 20-storey bungy jump inland from

Patong is built and operated to Kiwi standards. Jumpers have the option to dunk in the water, leap in pairs or experience the Rocket Man, where you'll be shot 50m into the air, then do the bungy thing on the way down.

LET'S RELAX *Spa*
☎ 076 346080; www.bloomingspa.com; 209/22-24 Th Rat Uthit; massages/wraps from 250/1000B; ⏱ 10.30am-midnight
The cool atrium, gushing with fountains, is infused with euca-

Sample the watersports menu at Hat Patong

lyptus and is the perfect place to devise your spa strategy. Will it be reflexology followed by a body scrub? Or would you rather a Thai herbal steam bath before a hot-stone massage and a facial? Life is full of tough decisions. Let's Relax has another spa at 121 Th Rat Uthit.

🏃 LONG-TAIL CHARTERS
Watersports
Nong Kwan Marine Rentals; Southern entrance to Th Thawiwong
To glimpse the sea from a different vantage point, consider a long-tail charter to beaches that aren't accessible by road. Freedom Beach (1500B return) is the most popular choice. But Laem Singh and Banana Rock Beach (4000B return), to the north, is even more remote.

🏃 NICKY'S HANDLEBAR
Adventure, Sports
☎ 076 345770; www.nickyshandlebar .com; 41 Th Rat Uthit; hire per day from 1200B
The tumbledown biker bar is a fun blast of *Easy Rider* nostalgia, but you're here to hire a Harley of your own. Kai and Nicky, the brothers behind this shop, have a sick showroom with a dozen big bikes. All of them hover around 1500cc, so these aren't for amateurs. You'll need a big bike license from your native land, but you won't need a map. Nicky and Kai have been

leading Harley tours in and around Phuket for a decade.

🏃 OCEAN BOWL PHUKET
Sports
Ocean Plaza Patong, Th Bangla; games 85B; ⏱ 2.30-11.30pm
On the top floor of this aging indoor mall is a decent bowling alley with a dozen lanes. If you come in flip-flops, you can hire shoes and socks. But it's probably best to bring your own cotton.

🏃 OCEAN DIVERS
Watersports
☎ 076 341273; www.oceanphuket.com; 142/6 Th Thawiwong
A veteran dive outfitter, Ocean Divers is Thai owned and operated and has been doing its thing since 1979. It offers live aboards to the Similan Islands, Ko Bon, Ko Tachai and Richelieu Rock, as well as day trips to Ko Racha Yai, Shark Point, King Cruiser Wreck and Ko Phi-Phi. And it has been recognised as a top eco-outfitter for its underwater garbage collection efforts.

🏃 PARAPHAT SEA SPORTS
CLUB *Watersports*
☎ 076 344632; www.phuketseasport .com; 141/11 Soi Royal Paradise; fishing trip for 4 people per day 19,000B, board hire per day 1200B, surf lesson per hr/2hr/4hr 300/1200/2000B

Diving is this club's bread and butter. It has day trips to Ko Racha Yai and Ko Racha Noi, Shark Point and Ko Phi-Phi, but it also offers deep-sea fishing trips for those after some black marlin, tuna and barracuda, and it hires boards and offers surfing instruction as well.

✈ PUM COOKING SCHOOL
Cooking Class
☎ 076 346269; www.pumthaifood chain.com; 204/32 Th Rat Uthit; class per person 2500B

This small restaurant chain (two locations in Thailand, two locations in France) conducts two four-hour classes every day at 11am and 4pm. Each class has a four-student limit and begins with a market tour and ends with a meal, and students leave with a recipe book.

✈ SCANDINAVIAN DIVERS
Watersports
☎ 076 294225; www.scandinavian -divers.com; 58/6 Soi Patong Resort; day trips from 2900B

Forget the name, this friendly dive outfitter located just off Th Bangla serves all. It does live aboards and day trips to Phi-Phi, Shark Point, Racha Yai and Racha Noi, and it also does a (long) day trip to the Similan Islands. But on its reasonable two-day, one-night

trip to the Similans you'll get seven dives.

✈ SCUBA CAT
Watersports
☎ 076 293120; www.scubacat.com; 94 Th Thawiwong; day trips from 3100B, live aboards from 28,700B

Live-aboard dive and kayak trips to the Similan and Surin Islands, all the courses you could want (including Technical diving), and day trips to Shark Point, Phi-Phi, Racha Yai and Racha Noi. This outfitter has been around for 15 years and gets rave reviews.

✈ SUNRISE DIVING
Watersports
☎ 076 292052; www.sunrisediving.net; 49 Th Thawiwong; day trips from 3500B, live aboards from 21,460B

One of Phuket's top dive schools, Sunrise offers all the courses you could possibly want – from Open Water to Digital Underwater Photography to Nitrox. And it has Similans and Richelieu Rock–bound live aboards, as well as half-day, two-dive trips to local reefs.

✈ SWASANA SPA *Spa*
☎ 076 340138; www.impiana.com; 41 Th Thawiwong; treatments from 850B; ☼ 9am-9pm

This four-star spa is right on the beach at the quiet north end

Treat yourself to a traditional Thai massage at Swasana Spa

of Patong. The best deal is the traditional Thai massage (850B). You'll be nestled in a cool glass cube on a cushy floor mat with ocean views.

🏃 WANG SAUNA Spa
☎ 081 2528068; Th Na Nai; treatments from 150B; ⏰ 10am-8pm
This newly established family-owned sauna on Patong's back streets honours the time-tested Thai tradition of aromatherapy. Inside the steam room the essence of wild ginger and lemon-grass will soothe your soul and extract any number of Patong-induced toxins.

🏃 WARM WATER DIVERS
Watersports
☎ 076 292201; www.warmwaterdivers .com; 227/229 Th Rat Uthit; day trips from 3000B, live aboards from 18,100B
One of the top dive outfitters on the island, Warm Water Divers offers all the courses and day trips (Racha Yai, Racha Noi Shark Point, King Cruiser, Anemone etc), but its live-aboard dive cruises

to the Similans are a cut above the rest thanks to the stunning Chinese wooden sailing ship, *The June Hong Chian Lee* (aka Respect Wind Travel Forever). It also leads half-day guided kayaking trips to remote and pristine beaches along the west coast, south of Patong.

☒ WATER WORLD ASIA
Watersports
☎ 076 3423511; www.waterworldasia .com; 189 Th Rat Uthit; day trips from 3100B
A well-heeled dive factory, Water World Asia offers an armada of dive boats, a full curriculum and a fantastic scuba shop.

SHOP
⌂ AMARIT *Design*
☎ 081 8941992; 99/2 Th Rat Uthit; ⌚ 6-11pm
This small but lovely art and antique shop is stocked with Thai paintings and Buddha sculpture. Definitely worth a look if you're contemplating converting your garden to Buddhism.

⌂ BAAN THAI ANTIQUES
Design, Homewares
☎ 076 292274; www.baanthai-antique .com; 80/5 Soi Permpong; ⌚ 10am-11pm
A glorious collection of antiques and new-production traditional

art from Myanmar (Burma), China, Laos and Thailand crowd this small shop. There are 70-year-old alabaster Buddhas, gongs, temple bells (the real thing), lacquer ware, ceramics, enormous doors and teak-wood reliefs. This place is not cheap, but serious collectors won't mind the expense of shopping at Baan Thai.

⌂ BAANBOONPITAK
Design, Homewares
☎ 076 341789; 30 Th Prachanukhro; ⌚ 10am-7pm
Ready for a treasure hunt? Hidden in this dusty antique shop is an array of teak sculpture, paintings, some excellent bronze work, massive buffalo-skin drums, bejewelled royal dogs and a lot of high-quality teak furniture. So get dirty and find something beautiful. The sardonically sweet shopkeeper will arrange shipping.

⌂ BANZAAN SHOPPING PLAZA *Market*
Behind Jung Ceylon
Banzaan has two faces. There are the tumbledown shopping stalls with your garden-variety knock offs and handicrafts if you're into bargain hunting, and the newly built fresh market. It's a posh version of a traditional Thai market, with a terrific seafood selection,

a food court upstairs and just enough funk to satisfy the soul.

📷 JUNG CEYLON *Mall*
Th Rat Uthit; 🕙 **10am-10pm**
Even the anticorporates among us will have to admit that this is a pretty cool mall. Yes, the major multinationals (Apple, Starbucks, Adidas, er, Dairy Queen) are well represented here, but the Sino-Phuket wing has a decent international restaurant row and the top-floor cinema is plush. Yet there is one small stall in a back corner that sells automatic weapons and flack jackets. No joke. That can't be a good sign for the future of humanity…or the Jung Ceylon.

📷 MANGO TREE *Beauty*
☎ **089 4753220; 245 Th Rat Uthit;** 🕙 **10am-11pm**
You can get a massage at this cute day spa, but the real stars are its branded, handmade spa products. The outdoor shelves are packed with glycerine bar soap, aromatherapy oils, lavender and mandarin bath crystals, and lemongrass shampoo and massage oil.

📷 MITSUKO *Fashion*
☎ **076 345132; 12 Th Bangla;** 🕙 **10am-10pm**
This branded shop is the brainchild of a French designer. Inside are boots, hip and splashy handbags, and belts encrusted with semiprecious stones, rivets, beads and shells.

📷 SIAM CERAMIC
Homewares
☎ **076 345103; www.thaibenjarong .com; 104/17-18 Soi Post Office;** 🕙 **9am-11pm**
Interested in elegant, hand-painted tea sets and table settings? Then you'll love this showroom. The translucent bone china teacups are rimmed with 18-carat gold.

📷 THE ROYAL KING COLLECTION
Fashion, Homewares
☎ **076 340180; royalkingin@gmall.com; 100/18 Soi Post Office;** 🕙 **10am-11pm**
This humble, Kashmiri-owned rug and textile shop stocks the best collection of carpets and pashminas on the island. OK, but who, you ask, buys fine wool in the tropics? Good point, but when you see deals this good, you don't check the thermometer, especially if you have winter at home. There are wools and silks of every colour and quality, from 100B to 4500B. Everything is handmade – some carpets, which can take years to make, cost US$10,000 and are still a bargain. The Royal King arranges all shipping in-house.

EAT

3 SPICES *Fusion* $$

☎ 076 340138; 41 Th Thawiwong;
🕑 11am-midnight
Welcome to well-dressed Asian fusion on the Patong strip. Enjoy miso and crab-meat soup and wok-fried snapper with coconut curry among other stellar dishes.

ALI BABA *Indian* $

☎ 076 345024; 38 Th Ruamchai;
🕑 11am-midnight
This cosy, spotless café serves tasty and traditional Indian food. It counts Patong's Indian residents among its loyal customers.

BAAN RIM PA *Thai* $$

☎ 076 344079; Th Kalim Beach;
🕑 11am-11pm
Stunning, classic Thai food is served with a side order of spectacular views at this long-time institution hanging over the cliffs of Kalim beach. Standards are high, with prices to match, but romance is in the air, with candlelight and piano music. Book ahead and consider ironing your shirt.

COCOA NUT *Thai* $

☎ 085 8880895; Th Rat Uthit;
🕑 1pm-2am
One of several street-side cafés and fish grills opposite the Royal Paradise. It serves a mean lobster, grilled or fried with garlic and pepper.

DANG RESTAURANT *Thai* $

☎ 076 344306; 188 Th Rat Uthit;
🕑 8am-midnight
Tasty local Thai food at insane prices. The wok-tossed chicken and basil, and fried crab curry are both wonderful, and it has 18 different fresh fruit smoothies. Its mango smoothie is the best on the island.

FLOYD'S BRASSERIE *French, Fusion* $$$

☎ 076 370000; www.burasari.com;
18/110 Th Ruamchai; 🕑 6-10.30pm; 🔗
One of England's favourite celebrity chefs, Keith Floyd, is the man behind the Burasari resort's popular restaurant. If duck breast braised in champagne, eggs poached in red wine and Phuket lobster thermidor gets you salivating, then this is your kind of place.

FRIED CHICKEN *Thai* $

163/5 Th Phra Barami; 🕑 10am-7pm;
🔗 👶
The name on the sign, though it is written in Thai script, doesn't lie. Three huge fryers are bubbling and splattering with juicy, crispy 'yard bird'. This establish-

ment is Muslim owned, so Halal doctrine dictates that it is clean. The chicken is served with a tangy hot sauce and sticky rice. It's impossible to overstate this: if you like fried chicken (all non-veggies raise your hand), this place is a must.

HOT CURRY *Indian* $$
☎ 076 292811; 206/22-23 Th Rat Uthit; 7.30am-midnight; V
There are bow-tied waiters and tablecloths at this spotless curry and tandoori house with an extensive vegetarian menu.

HUNG FAT'S *Chinese* $$$
☎ 076 290313; www.hungfats.com; 314 Th Phra Barami; 6.30pm-midnight, closed Mon
This eatery, the newest offering from those behind Baan Rim Pa restaurant group, serves dim sum and southern Szechuan Chinese cuisine garnished with live jazz. Brand new at the time of research, this spot was generating a tonne of buzz.

LIM'S *Thai* $$
☎ 076 344834; www.lim-thailand.com; Soi 7, 28 Th Phrabaramee; 6pm-midnight
Half a kilometre uphill from the coast road to Hat Kamala is this modern, moulded concrete dining room serving upscale Thai cuisine.

It serves papaya, pomelo and green mango salad; squid stir-fried with cashews; and roast duck in red curry sauce. When celebrities land in Phuket, most spend at least one evening here.

MENGRAI SEAFOOD *Thai* $
☎ 087 2637070; Soi Tun; 11am-11pm;
Located down a sweaty, dark *soi* (lane or small street) off Th Bangla is a wonderful food court serving fresh, local food. The stalls towards the end serve daily curries that local expats swear by. This restaurant specialises in fresh fish, prawns and mussels. The fish and vegetables are clearly very fresh.

NEWSPAPER *Thai* $$
☎ 076 346275; www.newspaper -phuket.com; 125/4-5 Soi Paradise Hotel; 24hr;
This designer boutique inn has a sweet, intimate dining room with woven rope chairs, roses on the tables, muslin-wrapped chandeliers and concrete floors. The menu is typical Thai, and it serves Western breakfasts.

PATONG FOOD PARK *Thai* $
Th Rat Uthit; 4pm-midnight;
Extending two blocks is this local foodie's dream world. There are five kinds of fresh fish, crab, lobster, roasted pork leg, satay

and *som tum* (green papaya salad) carts, and sticky rice with mango for dessert. All cheap and delicious.

🍴 SALA BUA *Fusion* $$$
☎ 076 340138; www.impiana.com; 41 Th Thawiwong; 🕑 6.30am-10.30pm
Enjoy award-winning Asian fusion cuisine in a seaside four-star resort setting. Start with the rock lobster, avocado, roasted vegetable and crayfish salad drizzled with a cognac vinaigrette and move on to the barramundi and mussels in crispy rice paper squares.

🍴 SAVOEY *Thai* $$
☎ 076 341171; 136 Th Thawiwong; 🕑 11am-11pm; 🚭 🚼
On an island packed with weighed-to-order fish grills, this is one of the best. Its huge ice shelf is packed with lobsters, prawns, grouper, red snapper, sole, trevally and barracuda. It also has live lobsters. It has one menu and four dining rooms – two of them on the sand. The food is always great, and the prices are quite reasonable.

🍴 TAKUMI *Japanese* $$
☎ 076 341654; Th Thawiwong; 🕑 1.30-11.30pm
This fantastic find, with the conspicuous Sumo mascot, specialises in *yakiniku* (Japanese

barbecue). You'll sit around granite tables embedded with hibachi broilers and self-cook crab, prawns, eel, squid and tenderloin sliced paper thin. Wash it down with one of the many varieties of cold sake. Takumi has a sushi menu, but broiling is its thing, so stick to what it does best.

🍴 TANTRA *Indian, English* $$
☎ 085 9099929; 186/5 Th Thawiwong; 🕑 11am-midnight; Ⓥ
Better dressed than Phuket's other Indian haunts, Tantra has cushioned floor seating and the usual array of dishes with some London pub grub mixed in. It also has a flat screen for all your fanatical cricket needs.

🍴 THE NINTH FLOOR
Steakhouse $$$
☎ 076 344311; www.the9thfloor.com; 47 Th Rat Uthit; 🕑 4pm-late
To get some perspective on just how massive Patong has become, come on up to the 9th floor of the Sky Inn Condotel building where you can watch the sea of lights spread through sliding-floor-to-ceiling glass doors. This rising star of Phuket's dining scene is the highest open-air restaurant on the island, but its ridiculously tender, perfectly prepared steaks and chops are what made it a Patong institution.

🍽 THE ORCHIDS *Thai* $
☎ 076 340462; 78/3-4 Th Thawiwong;
🕑 7am-11pm; 👶

Get your fantastic, cheap Thai food here. The beef *larb* (minced chicken, beef or pork salad mixed with chilli, mint and coriander) is scintillating and delicious, plus Orchids has all the curries and noodle dishes you love so well.

🍽 YEAN KOREAN BBQ
Korean $$$
☎ 076 340955; 210/4 Th Rat Uthit;
🕑 12.30-11.30pm

This small, tiled café leaves the grilling to you. Sizzle up thinly sliced beef, prawns or pork, and each dish comes with five kinds of

vegetables. Wash it down with a cold beer.

🍸 DRINK

🍸 I'M CAFFÉ *Café*
☎ 089 4639222; 138/33 Th Na Nai

The three major elements of a good indie coffee house – good tunes, better coffee and mood lighting – are all in effect at this local hang-out.

🍸 JP'S RESTAURANT & BAR
Lounge
☎ 076 343024; www.bydlofts.com; 5/28 Th Rat Uthit; 🕑 10.30am-11.30pm

This hipster indoor-outdoor lounge definitely brings a touch

Relax in the chic surrounds of JP's Restaurant & Bar

of style and panache to Patong. There's a low-slung bar, outdoor sofa booths that are cush, happy hour (with free tapas) from 10pm and weekly DJ parties.

🍸 LA GRITA *Lounge*
☎ 076 340106; www.amari.com; 2 Th Meun-ngern; ⏰ 10.30am-11.30pm
A spectacular, modern restaurant, La Grita doesn't fit with the aging bones of this once great property, but who cares? With tiered booths, massive yet muted light boxes and a deck just centimetres above the boulder-strewn shore, there's no better place for a sunset cocktail.

🍸 MONTE'S *Pub*
Th Phisit Karani; ⏰ 11am-midnight
Now this, my friends, is a tropical pub. It has a thatched roof, a natural wood bar, dozens of orchids and a flat screen for sports games. The barflies swarm on Fridays for Monte's famous Belgian-style mussels, and on weekends he fires up the grill.

🍸 TWO BLACK SHEEP *Pub*
☎ 089 8722645; 172 Th Rat Uthit; ⏰ 11am-2am
Owned by a fun Aussie couple (he's a musician, she's a chef), this old-school pub is a great find. They have good grub and live music nightly. From 8pm to 10pm there's an acoustic set, then Chilli Jam, the

CONNECT FOUR!
Is it just an innocent children's game or a bar girl's ruse to get you to hand her your cash 100B at a time? You'll find out on Th Bangla (see p21). After all, it seems an innocent enough pastime when you belly up to the bar. You'll play a game or two with a beautiful woman for a few hundred baht while you sip another Singha. But know that your opponent is a Connect Four mastermind. She will win, quickly and easily. You'll go for double or nothing. Your friends will help you strategise. And she'll win again. Even easier this time. Be afraid. Be very afraid.

house band, gets up and rocks till last call. Towards the wee hours local musicians, fresh off their gigs, filter in and spontaneous jams ensue. And they ban bar girls, which keeps everything rated PG.

⭐ PLAY
🟦 BANGLA BOXING STADIUM *Stadium*
☎ 072 822348; Th Bangla; admission general/ringside 1300/1500B; ⏰ 9-11.30pm Tue, Wed, Fri & Sun
This punch-drunk fight club feels like the kind of place Rocky was discovered at before he got his long shot. But it also happens to be the top stadium in Phuket. It has bouts four nights a week, and each fight card usually has nine bouts. Your bloodlust will be sated here.

⭐ CLUB LIME *Club*
☎ 085 7981850; www.clublime.info;
🕑 10pm-2am
A new hot spot gaining steam, this place attracts the beautiful people and a rotating roster of Thai and international DJs.

⭐ ROCK CITY *Club*
Th Kalim Beach; admission free;
🕑 6pm-2am
Let the grunge begin! This dark den of rock lives on the glory of cover bands. There's live music nightly, there are AC DC, Metallica and GnR tribute bands, and other rockers who channel the Chili Peppers, the Stones and Bon Jovi in one show. Free entry before 11pm, so get there early and keep it rockin'.

⭐ SAXOPHONE
Restaurant, Club
Th Kalim Beach; admission free;
🕑 6pm-midnight
Down the block from Rock City is this candle-lit jazz and blues dining room, with Mississippi Delta décor and live jazz nightly.

⭐ SEDUCTION *Club*
www.seductiondisco.com; 39/1 Th Bangla; admission 500B; 🕑 10pm-4am
Patong's newest and most popular dance hall comes courtesy of a Finnish club impresario. Known for buying up Helsinki's best clubs, he opened this one in 2006 and has since attracted international party people dancing to well-known global DJs. Design, lighting and sound system are all top shelf. The club opens before midnight, but the party doesn't start rocking till the wee small hours.

⭐ SIMON CABARET *Theatre*
☎ 076 342011; www.phuket-simon cabaret.com; Th Sirirach; admission 550B
About 300m south of town is a drag cabaret that even the staunchest hetero would love. The 600-seat theatre is grand, production value is high, the costumes are gorgeous and the ladyboys are, well, quite ladylike. Performances begin at 7.30pm and 9.30pm nightly – book ahead.

>HAT KARON & HAT KATA

Separated by a slim headland, these two west-coast beaches have very different personalities. Kata, to the south, has excellent dining options, some quite upscale. It's also backed by a rim of trees, has offshore island views and is downright gorgeous. It's younger and more energetic than Karon, which is long, languid and much calmer.

Both beaches are beautiful and attract families and package tourists from Europe. In fact, there's a solid chance that during the high season Scandinavian tourists outnumber local Thais, which explains why the beach boys speak Swedish, and meatballs and mashed potatoes can be found on more than a few menus.

HAT KARON & HAT KATA

◉ SEE
Wat Karon **1** C1

🏃 DO
Aspasia **2** B3
Body@Mind **3** C3
Calypso Divers **4** C3
Dino Park **5** B3
Dive Asia **6** C1
Dive Asia **7** C3
Jet Hat Karon **8** B2
Jet Ski Hat Kata **9** C5
Longtail Charters **10** C5
Marina Divers **11** B1
Mom Tri's Cooking
    Class .... (see 42)
Parasailing Hat Kata ...**12** C5
Phuket Scuba Club **13** C5
Phuket Surf **14** C5
Scuuba Doo **15** B3
Siam Arokaya **16** B1
Spa Royale **17** C5
Sunrise Divers **18** C3
Thailand Tours &
    Paradise Golf..........(see 30)

The Royal Spa **19** B1
The Sense Spa **20** C5

🛍 SHOP
Bookazine.....................**21** C3
One Man Gift Shop **22** C1
Rattana Kosini..............**23** C5
Siam Handicrafts..........**24** C3

🍴 EAT
Best Friend
    Restaurant **25** B3
Capannina **26** C5
Casa Pizza.....................**27** C5
Dome **28** C4
Everest Kitchen **29** C4
Great Curries of India ...**30** B1
Gung.............................**31** C5
Kampong-Kata Hill Restaurant
    & Galleria.................**32** C4
Karon Seafood..............**33** C1
Kata Café **34** C5
Little Mermaid **35** B1
Mama Noi's...................**36** C2
Mom Tri's Kitchen........**37** C5

Nanta............................**38** C5
Oyster **39** C5
Tapas & Wine...............**40** C5
Thai Kitchen **41** C3
The Boathouse **42** C5
The Pad Thai Shop........**43** C3

🍸 DRINK
10's Coffee....................**44** C1
After Beach Bar **45** D6
Angus O'Toole's...........**46** B1
Beach Club....................**47** C6
Coco Palm.....................**48** C5
Italian Job.....................**49** C5
Las Margaritas..............**50** B1

⭐ PLAY
Candlelight Bar **51** C3
Kata Grill Garden..........**52** C4
Ratri Jazztaurant..........**53** C4

KARON

Th Vitat

Hat Karon

Th Kata (Patak West)

Th Patak East

Ao Karon

Th Thai Na

Post Office

Laem Sai

Th Ked Kwan

Ko Pu

Hat Kata Yai

KATA

Ao Kata Yai

To Big Buddha

Th Koktanod (Patak West)

Th Kata (Patak West)

Th Koktanod (Patak West)

Hat Kata Noi

Th Kata Sai Yuan

Th Kata Noi

Ao Kata Noi

4233

To Nai Han-Rawai; Promthep Cape;
Karon View Point; Tassani Beach;
Kok Chang Safari

0   1 km
0   0.6 miles

HAT KARON

Even with two megaresorts and package tourists aplenty, Hat Karon has more sand space per capita than Patong or Kata. On the northernmost edge, accessible from a rutted road that extends past the vendors and food stalls, the beach tucks into a headland. That's Karon's sweet spot, and the water is like turquoise glass. From the north, the beach extends down in a gentle arc before curling again into another turquoise and gold crescent at the south end. Within the network of streets and plazas behind the beach you'll find a blend of good local food, more Scandinavian signage than seems reasonable and a lovely temple. Unlike Kata, which is fairly compact, Karon sprawls a bit, which helps mute that dose of Patong sleaze that lurks on the back roads.

👁 SEE
👁 WAT KARON
Th Patak East; admission free
Set back from the road is a relatively new temple complex with a small shine occupied by a seated, black-stone Buddha. Behind it is the striking crematorium with its tiered roof – which only opens on ceremonial days. The grounds are lush with banana, palm and mango trees.

🏃 DO
🏃 BODY@MIND *Spa*
☎ 076 398274; www.body-mindspa .com; 558/7-12 Th Patak West; massages/ spa packages from 600/1200B
A nice 'tweener. It's more upscale than the shopfront spas and not as pricey as the resort spas. It has a full menu of massages, wraps, scrubs and half-day packages, and it provides a free round-trip transfer from your hotel.

🏃 DINO PARK
Amusement Park
☎ 076 330625; www.dinopark.com; Th Patak West; adult/child 240/180B; 🕙 10am-midnight
Jurassic Park meets minigolf at this bizarre park on the southern edge of Hat Karon. It's a maze of caves, lagoons, leafy gardens, dinosaur statues and, of course, putting greens. Kids will dig it the most.

🏃 DIVE ASIA *Watersports*
☎ 076 330598; www.diveasia.com; 24 Th Patak West; day trips from 3100B
Considered by many to be the best outfitter in Karon, Dive Asia hits the southern reefs (Ko Racha Yai and Ko Racha Noi, Shark Point, Anemone Reef and Ko Phi-Phi), teaches a full curriculum of classes, and has liveaboard options to the Similan and Surin Islands. (Note: there are two Dive Asia locations in Hat Karon.)

⚡ JET SKI HAT KARON
Watersports
Hat Karon; per 30min 1500B
Like nearly all the west-coast beaches, you can skim the sea on a jet ski at Hat Karon.

⚡ MARINA DIVERS *Watersports*
☎ 076 330272; www.marinadivers.com; 45 Th Karon; day trips from 2700B
It has a nice selection of day trips to Phuket's outlying reefs, as well as a long day trip to the Similan Islands. No one else in Karon does that.

⚡ SCUUBA DOO *Watersports*
☎ 076 333606; www.scuubadoo.com; 25 Th Karon; day trips from 3100B
The name is what it is. Ignore it. Because it has a solid dive curriculum and daily dives to Phuket's go-to reefs.

⚡ SIAM AROKAYA *Spa*
☎ 079 292474; 6 Th Thayna; treatments/ spa packages from 300/500B; ⏲ 11am-10pm
Here is a shopfront spa with a little panache. You can pamper

T-Rex meets putting green at Dino Park

yourself with a seaweed, milk and pineapple body scrub, a herbal steam and a facial with a green-tea mask. Or just pick from any of its 10 massage varieties.

⚓ SUNRISE DIVERS
Watersports
☎ 076 398040; www.sunrise-divers
.com; 269/24 Th Patak East; live aboards from 24,000B
The biggest live-aboard agent in Phuket, it can book passage on boats to the Similan Islands ranging from backpacker grunge to sweet luxury.

🏌 THAILAND TOURS & PARADISE GOLF *Sports*
☎ 084 8433677; www.golfinphuket
.com; Centara Mall, Th Patak East; custom trips varying prices
Swedish owned and operated, it arrange custom-golf and deep-sea fishing trips for independent travellers. If you are into golf, these guys are the island's authority.

🏃 THE ROYAL SPA *Spa*
☎ 076 286464; 206 Th Karon; treatments from 1850B; ☉ 10am-8pm
Part of the Sea Sands Resort, this four-star spa delivers both luxury and therapy. It has a nice selection of Thai treatments, but also offers Ayurvedic and hot-stone massage.

🛍 SHOP
📘 BOOKAZINE *Books*
☎ 076 333273; 23/7 Th Karon;
☉ 10am-11pm
If you need more beach reading, you will find a wealth of English-language titles, from bestsellers to regional fiction and nonfiction, at this local chain.

🎁 ONE MAN GIFT SHOP *Gifts*
☎ 076 396267; 601 Moo 1, Th Patak;
☉ 10am-11pm
This tiny shop has a nice collection of quintessential Thai woodcarvings. There's nothing groundbreaking here, but the selection is good and so are the prices.

🍴 EAT
🍽 BEST FRIEND RESTAURANT
Thai $$
☎ 019 682398; 2 Moo 3, Th Patak West;
☉ 11am-11pm; 🚸
One of several tasty Thai seafood cafés on the beach road, Best Friend serves routinely good food, and at night it displays its fresh fish and wine in ice-filled steel rafts. It's an appetising look.

🍽 GREAT CURRIES OF INDIA
Indian $
Centara Mall, 514/11 Th Patak; ☉ 11am-11pm; Ⓥ
It isn't lying. The wide range of curries at this family-owned café is

fantastic. It also has tasty kebabs, tandoori chicken and fish tikka. Take it away or dine in and enjoy the ever-strobing sounds and images of Bollywood.

🍴 KARON SEAFOOD *Thai* $$

☎ 076 396797; 514 Moo 1, Th Patak East; ⏲ 11am-11pm; Ⓥ ♿

This place is definitely not off the beaten track, but sometimes that's OK. Hordes descend for delicacies like sliced fish in green curry, and squid with basil and chilli. It also has a menu with 10 vegetarian items.

🍴 LITTLE MERMAID
Thai, European $$

631 Soi Mermaid; ⏲ 11am-11pm; 💻 ♿

With menus in six languages, free wi-fi, hearty Western breakfasts and evening barbecues, you're likely to have at least one meal here if you're sleeping in Karon. There are lamb chops on Monday, ribs on Wednesday and Phuket lobster on Saturday nights.

🍴 MAMA NOI'S *Thai, Italian* $

☎ 076 286272; Karon Plaza, 291/1-2 Moo 3, Th Patak East; ⏲ 8am-11pm; ♿

Repeat visitors adore this place, which churns out fantastic Thai and Italian pasta dishes. It does a superb *gaeng som* (southern Thai curry with fish and prawns),

it bakes its own baguettes every morning and it has the best banana shake on the island.

🍴 THE PAD THAI SHOP *Thai* $

Th Patak East; ⏲ 8am-3pm

On the busy main road behind Karon, just north of the tacky Ping Pong Bar, is this glorified food stand that spills from the owners' home onto a dirt lot. It's only open for lunch, when you can find chicken-feet stew, beef-bone soup and the best *pàt tai* (Thai fried noodles, usually with peanuts) on planet Earth. Spicy and sweet, packed with prawns, tofu, egg and peanuts, and wrapped in a fresh banana leaf, you will be grateful.

🍸 DRINK

🍸 10'S COFFEE *Café*

☎ 076 398474; 489 Th Patak East; ⏲ 8am-10pm; 💻

There's a terrific selection of gourmet coffee, teas and fresh fruit shakes at this new café. You can sit inside or out and it has a computer set up for free internet.

🍸 ANGUS O'TOOLES *Pub*

Centara Mall, Th Patak; ⏲ 10am-midnight

This proper Irish pub has all the cricket and rugby matches on its flat screen and Guinness and Kilkenny on tap.

LAS MARGARITAS
Bar
528/7 Th Patak East; 🕙 **11am-11pm**
Where else can you get carne asada, chicken marsala, fettuccine alfredo, Thai stir-fry and New York cheesecake all in the same place? Thankfully nowhere. But it does have tasty margaritas and a terrace with sea views upon which to enjoy them.

⭐ PLAY
⭐ CANDLELIGHT BAR
Bar, Music Venue
Karon Plaza, 291/1-2 Moo 3, Th Patak
Tucked into a small corner of Karon Plaza is this dive courtyard bar furnished with timber tables, and decorated with beads, shells and coral. It's the perfect venue for a reggae band, which it hosts every Tuesday night. Sunday nights are for country music. Shirts optional. Live music starts at 9.30pm.

HAT KATA

Kata makes for a fun base from which to explore the rest of Phuket. The beach is stunning and alive with tourists of all ages. It offers surfing in the shoulder and wet seasons when the swell arrives, some terrific day spas and fantastic food. The beach is actually divided in two by a rocky headland, and the road between them is home to Phuket's original millionaire's row. Hat Kata Yai is on the north end, while the more secluded Hat Kata Noi unfurls to the south. Both offer soft golden sand and attract a bohemian (read: topless sunbathing) crowd. Not that there's anything wrong with that.

👁 SEE
 BIG BUDDHA
off Hwy 402, north of Chalong Circle; admission free
Phuket's newest monument, this massive, alabaster stone Buddha is scheduled to be complete in 2010, but it's already an awe-inspiring sight, offering spiritual energy and spectacular views to match. For more information, see opposite and p13.

👁 **KARON VIEW POINT**
Hwy 4233; admission free
Further along the highway from After Beach Bar (p82) is this majestic viewpoint. From here, your view extends from the northern reaches of Karon to the Phromthep Cape. Come for sunset. But don't linger late at night. There have been attacks and robberies in the wee hours (see boxed text, p86).

 Kun Suporn Wanichakul
Director of the Big Buddha Project

How much will it cost and how long will it take to build this Big Buddha?
We started in 2002, and I project that we will finish in 2010. It's a 60 million
baht project and when we are finished it will be the biggest Buddha in the
world. **What do you think the Buddha and this location will do for those
who visit?** I hope it brings good to them, and I think when people come
here they will gain some insight into their lives, understand what makes
them unhappy and hopefully begin to educate themselves about Buddha's
teachings. **Do you meditate?** I have meditated every day for 25 years. When
you look outside yourself you can become jealous or angry and unhappy.
When you meditate, you train yourself to look within and listen to your
heart, and this makes you happy.

V

BEACHES & TOWNS

HAT KARON & HAT KATA

SHUT UP AND SMILE
When the Buddha sat in silence under that bodhi tree all those years ago, he was practising Vipassana meditation, the preferred method in Thailand's Theravada Buddhist tradition. Everything else, the chanting, the scripture, the candles and incense came later, and actually, according to the Buddha, has nothing to do with reaching enlightenment. Only meditation matters.

Vipassana grew to international prominence when SN Goenka used it to rehabilitate violent inmates in Indian prisons. Today inner-peace seekers willing to sit down and shut up for 10 days can check into Vipassana centres all over the world for free. Locals who practise Vipassana consider it vital to the cultivation of personal happiness. If you're looking to tame your monkey mind, you'll find the meditation centre at Big Buddha monument (p74 and p13), where resident monks will teach you the basics.

🚶 DO

🧖 ASPASIA Spa
☎ 076 333033; www.aspasiaphuket.com; 1/3 Th Laem Sai; treatments from 1000B; ⏰ 9am-9pm
A brilliant day spa option is hidden away at this unique condo resort on the headland between Kata and Karon. The interior is cosy and very Zen with sliding rice-paper doors dividing the treatment rooms. Try the red sweet body scrub, a mixture of sesame, honey and fresh orange juice. Or maybe you'd rather the coconut and passionfruit exfoliation? It also has a full-service beauty salon and offers a variety of massage styles.

🏊 CALYPSO DIVERS
Watersports
☎ 076 330869; www.calypsophuket.com; 84 Th Thai Na; dive trips from 3600B

With Calypso, Kata's best dive outfitter, you can hit all the reefs. It offers enough courses to make you a dive master, and three boats that sail to dive sites near and far daily. Nitrox is available here as well.

🏄 JET SKI HAT KATA
Watersports
near the main entrance to Hat Kata; per 30min/1hr 1500/2800B
Lion, the dreadlocked, devout Thai Hindu Rasta will hook you up with a jet ski so you, too, can buzz Ao Kata. If you call ahead, he can deliver the water hogs to Hat Kata Noi as well.

🐘 KOK CHANG SAFARI
Animal Interaction
☎ 089 5919413; 287 Moo 2, Hwy 4233; tours from 600B; ⏰ 8.30am-5.30pm
This well-run, attractive elephant camp is easily one of the best in

Phuket – if not the best. (Most importantly, the animals here are healthy.) Tours last 20 minutes to an hour. If you do the full hour (1000B), you'll have a magical view from the top of the mountain. Or you could always ditch the elephants and have a drink with Charlie, a friendly and damn handsome monkey. He'll be at the bar.

✈ LONGTAIL CHARTERS
Watersports
near the main entrance to Hat Kata; per half-day 5000B
Full- and half-day charters are available to Coral island and Ko Bon from Hat Kata.

✈ MOM TRI'S COOKING CLASS *Cooking Classes*
☎ 076 330015; www.boathousephuket .com; Th Patak West; 2 classes incl lunch 3200B; ⏰ 10am-1pm Sat & Sun
The Boathouse's award-winning executive chef, Tummanoon Punchun, carves a bit of time out of his schedule to teach the basics of Thai cooking. Class takes place just off the Boathouse dining room (p81), so you will cook with a view. For more information, see p24.

✈ PARASAILING HAT KATA
Watersports
near the main entrance to Hat Kata; per trip 1000B

As at Jet Ski Hat Kata (p77), Lion is once again the man to see. He will harness you in for 10 minutes of flying. That's enough time to loop the whole bay.

✈ PHUKET SCUBA CLUB
Watersports
☎ 076 284026; www.phuket-scuba -club.com; 241 Th Koktanod; local dives from 1000B, full day trips from 2900B
This ecologically sensitive outfitter has a shop here and another on Karon. It can arrange day trips to Racha Yai and Racha Noi Shark Point et al, as well as live aboards to the Similan Islands, and it's the only shop in the area to offer two beach dives from Hat Karon daily (11am and 3pm). The visibility isn't as magical as more distant reefs, but there are interesting fish around, plus it's close, so you'll be able to slip underwater and be back with the family in no time.

✈ PHUKET SURF
Watersports
☎ 081 0022496; www.phuketsurf.com; Th Koktanod; lessons from 1500B
Based at Hat Kata Yai's southern cove, the island's surf authority hires boards and offers surf lessons. Check its website for more info about the local surfing community and for morning surf reports.

⚑ SPA ROYALE *Spa*
☎ 076 333568; www.villaroyalephuket
.com; 12 Th Kata Noi; treatments from
1200B; ⏰ 9am-8pm
With organic spa products, seaside
treatment rooms and highly
skilled therapists, this is one of the
top spas in southern Phuket. Its
90-minute aromatherapy massage
is an all-timer.

⚑ THE SENSE SPA *Spa*
☎ 076 333014; www.thesensespa.com;
2/12 Kata Plaza, Th Kata Sua Yuan;
treatments from 750B; ⏰ 10am-10pm
Seeking a step up from the
street-spa vibe? Then get your
yourself into the plush environs of
this addictive day spa. There are
facials with aloe and honey, and
a coffee scrub with milk and shea

nut butter, among other luxurious
treatments, not to mention a full
massage menu.

🛍 SHOP

⬛ RATTANA KOSINI
Fashion, Design
203 Th Patak West; ⏰ 10am-11.30pm
Lost in a huddle of tiny tourist
trinket traps, Rattana Kosini is a
more dignified boutique. It has
nice tapestries, folk art, sculpture,
jewellery, and skirts and blouses
at reasonable prices. It's definitely worth a peek.

⬛ SIAM HANDICRAFTS
Fashion
☎ 076 333186; 27 Th Thai Na;
⏰ 10am-11pm

KATA VISIONARY

There's nobody more responsible for Phuket's tourism boom than Harvard educated architect Mom Luang Tri Devakul, known simply as Mom Tri (see p140). The wine aficionado with royal bloodlines first bought land and built a house on the bluff between Hat Kata Yai and Hat Kata Noi in the 1970s. At the time there were no regular commercial flights to Phuket from Bangkok, and very little development on the island. That changed when he designed the Club Med resort.

Club Med's investment inspired Thai Air to begin daily flights to Phuket, and more development followed, much of which Mom Tri invested in and designed, including the Royal Phuket Yacht Club, Le Meridian Phuket Beach Resort and Mom Tri's The Boathouse (p81), a boutique resort on Kata with a restaurant that became the first in Thailand to win the Wine Spectator Magazine Award of Excellence. Today his original home, accented by a fantastic art collection, is his newest boutique hotel property, Villa Royale.

All of his work shows his ability to adapt to and incorporate a site's natural features rather than bulldoze over them, which is often the cheaper and more popular choice. This is especially true at Hat Kata, where he preserved the canopy that gives it a feeling of magical seclusion.

Here's your hippie-wear super-store. The linen clothes are hand-made from hemp and organic cotton, and it has a lovely collection of silver and beaded jewellery.

 # EAT

🍴 CAPANNINA
Italian $$

☎ 076 284318; capannina@fastmail.fm; 30/9 Moo 2, Th Kata; 🕙 11am-midnight; **V** 👶

The chefs at this hip, open-air bistro with moulded concrete booths and imported olive oil on the tables start prepping early in the day. Everything here – from the pasta dishes to the sauces – is made fresh. It gets crowded during the high season, so you may want to book ahead.

🍴 CASA PIZZA
Italian $

211 Th Patak West; 🕙 11am-11pm; **V**

This hole-in-the-wall pizzeria with a knotted wood bar and creased tablecloths serves spring rolls, ice-cream sundaes and 28 varieties of thin-crust, wood-fired pizza – from Hawaiian to *diavolo* to gorgonzola.

🍴 DOME *Thai* $
☎ 076 330270; www.domeresort phuket.com; 98 Moo 4, Hat Kata Yai; 🕙 8am-10pm; 👶

This humble bungalow resort has cheap and delicious traditional Thai fare. Servings are a bit small, but are perfectly prepared. It does a brisk lunch business among local businessmen.

🍴 EVEREST KITCHEN
Nepalese $

☎ 084 6291721; 105 Th Ked Kwan; 🕙 11am-11pm

If you're taking a night off curry and grilled seafood, try this sweet Nepalese-owned café. It has hookah pipes and some damn good lamb tikka marsala.

🍴 GUNG
Fusion $$$

☎ 076 333568; 2/2 Moo 2, Th Patak West; 🕙 noon-11pm

The esteemed Mom Tri group's latest addition to Kata dining is this laid-back Asian fusion spot right on the beach. Sip some mango gazpacho and nibble on sesame-crusted *ahi* or steamed local sea bass, and between courses enjoy the eye-opening passion-fruit sorbet while you watch the oblong paper lanterns swing in the trees.

🍴 KAMPONG-KATA HILL RESTAURANT & GALLERIA
Thai $$

☎ 076 330103; Th Patak West; 🕙 noon-10pm

Dine with the sand between your toes at Gung (p79)

Choc-a-block with weathered Thai antiques and serving some fabulous local dishes, this excellent little eatery is up a long, creaky stairway. Your rewards are great views and some terrific Thai seafood.

🍴 KATA CAFÉ *Thai* $

Sugar Plum mall, Th Kata; ⏲ **11am-11pm**
The less glamorous cousin of the swanky Mali on the street side of the Sugar Plum mall serves deli-cious, affordable Thai favourites and boasts a tasty fish grill for dinner. Pluck your prawns, snapper and calamari from the ice and enjoy the free salad bar while you wait. If you're on a budget, this is one of the best-value options in Kata.

🍴 MOM TRI'S KITCHEN
Mediterranean, Thai $$$
☎ 076 330015; Th Kata Noi;
⏲ 6.30am-midnight

Another fine link in the Boathouse chain, the intimate Mom Tri's Kitchen offers fusion *haute cuisine* and fine wines, while diners overlook breathtaking Hat Kata Noi.

🍴 NANTA

Southeast Asian $$$

☎ 076 284760; www.malisavillas.com; 40/36 Th Kata; 🕑 8am-11pm

This drop-dead gorgeous villa property is hidden a bit from Kata proper, but is worth seeking out. The restaurant – with its aged teak floors and tables – offers hits from Thailand, Malaysia and Indonesia, as well as steaks and chops.

🍴 OYSTER

Thai, Chinese $$

☎ 076 333583; Th Kata; 🕑 11am-midnight

Choose your seafood from the ice raft and it will be shelled, steamed, grilled or wok fried in no time. Dishes are prepared in both Thai and Chinese styles, and the restaurant has a terrific island bar if all you need is a little lubrication.

🍴 TAPAS & WINE

Thai, European $$

☎ 084 382685; www.tapasandwinephuket.com; 98/8 Moo 4, Th Kata; 🕑 5-11pm

Swedish meatballs? Check. Veggie spring rolls? Uh huh. Spanish olives? Yessir. And you can pair this wide range of delicious tapas with an enviable wine selection. Come on a Monday night and see Elvis next door.

🍴 THAI KITCHEN *Thai* $

☎ 076 330157; 110/4 Kata Centre, Th Thai Na; 🕑 11am-10pm Sun-Fri

Thai Kitchen serves up steaming bowls of curry, pungent soup and an array of daily specials. Its menu includes pumpkin and prawns, braised eggplant with prawns, and boiled eggs with coriander and tamarind sauce. There's a brunch buffet – that's when the locals flock here. From 2pm onward, you'll have to order off the menu.

🍴 THE BOATHOUSE

Mediterranean Fusion $$$

☎ 076 330015; www.boathousephuket.com; Th Patak West; 🕑 7am-midnight

The Boathouse has been the critic's champion for some time. It's made all the hot lists (including *Wine Spectator*'s), and with good reason. The Mediterranean fusion food is fabulous (think vodka-marinated lobster and foie gras with black-truffle oil), the wine list is endless and the sea views are sublime. It's a fancy place – this is the closest Phuket

BEACHES & TOWNS

HAT KARON & HAT KATA

The drinks aren't the only things to savour at After Beach Bar

gets to old-school dining – so break out the smell goods and do your best to blend in. Sunburned dudes in tank tops tend to be a little conspicuous. Book ahead to secure a table close to the sand, and save room for the rich, silky chocolate soufflé.

DRINK

AFTER BEACH BAR *Bar*
☎ 081 8943750; Hwy 4233;
🕐 11am-midnight
It's difficult, make that impossible, to overstate how glorious the view is from this stilted, thatched, patio bar hanging off a cliff above Kata. Think 180-degree views of the sea, rocky peninsulas and layered palm-dappled hills. Now turn on the Bob Marley and you've got the best reggae bar in Phuket. The menu is packed with northern and southern Thai faves, at sunset the sky performs a light show, and when the fireball finally drops, the lights of fishing boats blanket the horizon. Not bad at all.

BEACH CLUB *Bar*
☎ 076 330124; www.katathani.com;
14 Th Kata Noi
This mod, stylish beach bar is courtesy of the Katahthani, a glitzy megaresort that dominates Hat Kata Noi.

ⓨ COCO PALM *Bar*

☎ 076 330530; www.katagroup/kata
beach.com; 1 Th Pakbang; ⏰ noon-11pm
Situated left of the main entrance
to Hat Kata and part of the massive Kata Beach Resort, this pool-
side café and bar is a great spot for
a happy-hour sundowner.

ⓨ ITALIAN JOB
Café

179/1 Th Koktanod; ⏰ 7am-9pm; 💻
This hip coffee lounge has wi-fi,
decent pastries, delicious Italian
espresso and a loyal morning
following.

⭐ PLAY

⭐ KATA GRILL GARDEN
Music Venue

☎ 076 330269; 98/7 Moo 4, Th Kata;
admission free; ⏰ 11am-11pm

You aren't here to eat. You've
come for Thai Elvis. He's a young
Elvis – round about when he
first discovered the power of his
pelvis. But his deep, velvet croon
deserves a better sound system.
Unfortunately, he doesn't stick
to the Elvis songbook, but when
he does the place goes wild. Elvis
enters the building at 9pm on
Mondays.

⭐ RATRI JAZZTAURANT
Bar, Lounge

☎ 076 333538; Th Chalong-Karon;
admission free; ⏰ 11am-1am
If you like jazz, you should wind
your way up to this hillside terrace
to listen to local and international
acts blow like they mean it. It's
especially sweet at sunset, and the
food comes highly recommended
as well.

>RAWAI

Now this is a place to live. Phuket's rapidly developing south coast is teeming with retirees, Thai and expat entrepreneurs, and a service sector that, for the most part, moved here from somewhere else.

The attraction is obvious. Think beautiful beaches and steep coastal hills that tumble into the Andaman Sea forming Laem Phromthep, Phuket's southernmost point.

Hat Nai Han, with its bobbing yachts, seafront temple and tremendous monsoon-season surf break, is the best beach in the area (see p19) and one of the best in Phuket, but there are smaller, hidden beaches that are just as beautiful. And Hat Rawai, a rocky harbour for long tails and speedboats, is studded with locally owned grills with delicious fresh seafood.

Plus, though Rawai is on the southern edge, it's actually the most central location on the island. From here it's just 15 minutes to Phuket City, five minutes to Kata and 20 minutes to Patong, which is why most visitors book holiday homes and plan to stay a while.

RAWAI

👁 SEE
Aikan Art 1 D1
Ao Sane 2 B2
Hat Ya Noi.....................3 C3
Laem Phromthep 4 C4
Red Gallery 5 D2
Romadon Gallery 6 E1
Secret View Point...........7 C3
Wat Nai Han 8 C2

🏃 DO
Atsumi Healing..............9 E1
Boat Charters 10 D3
Hat Rawai 11 E3
Herbal Steam Sauna.....12 D1
Phuket Elephant Ride...13 C1

Phuket Paradise 4WD
  Tour ....(see 13)
Rawai Muay Thai..........14 E1

🛍 SHOP
BZenter 15 D1

🍽 EAT
Arlecchino Homemade
  Ice Cream................(see 15)
Baan Rimlay 16 E3
Bleu Blanc Grill............17 D1
Chao Khun...................18 D1
Da Vinci ....(see 15)
Don's Cafe...................19 D1
German Bakery.............20 D2

Kitchen Grill................21 D2
La Chaumiere 22 D1
Lobster Restaurant 23 C3
Rawai Night Market.....24 E1
Rawai Seafood Grills.....25 E3
Roti House...................26 D1
Rum Jungle 27 D1
Som Tum Lanna............28 E1

🍸 DRINK
Coffee@Home 29 E1
Freedom Pub................30 E3
Nikita's ....(see 16)
The Royal Phuket
  Yacht Club 31 C2
VW Bar.......................32 D1

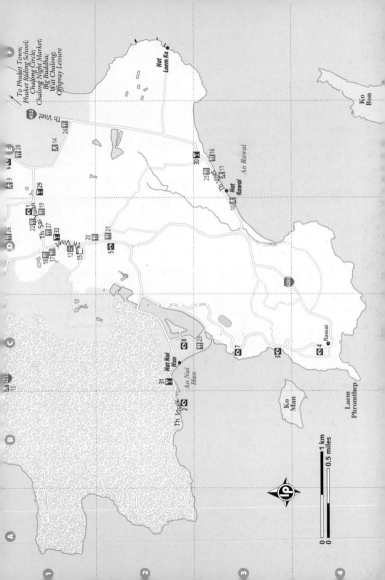

To Phuket Town;
Phuket Riding School;
Chalong Circle;
Chalong Night Market;
Big Buddha;
Wat Chalong;
Offspray Leisure

Th Viset

Hat
Leem Ka

28

14

24

30

25

16

Ao Rawai

11

Hat
Rawai

10

9

29

19

21

Th Viset

1

22

27

26

32

18

12 15

20

5

Th Viset

17

31

Hat Nai
Harn

8

7

23

Ao Nai
Harn

31

Th Viset

2

Rawai

4

3

Ko
Man

Laem
Phromthep

Ko
Bon

1 km
0.5 miles

N
S

0
0

BEACHES & TOWNS

RAWAI

👁 SEE

👁 AIKAN ART

☎ 084 8445593; 46/9 Th Sai Yuan; admission free; ⏲ 10am-7pm

Aikan, the 35-year-old artist, paints lovely depictions of Buddha and some terrific village landscapes. He is commissioned regularly and charges up to 15,000B for a single canvas.

👁 AO SANE

Moo 1, north of The Royal Phuket Yacht Club; admission free

From Hat Nai Han it appears as if the road dead-ends into the yacht club. Not true. Keep following the road through the underground parking structure and it pops out on the other side and continues to a small but beautiful, boulder-strewn white-sand beach (see p19).

👁 HAT YA NOI

Hwy 4233; admission free

Tucked between Hat Nai Han and Laem Phromthep, where the road dips back down to the sea, is this lovely cove with a healthy rock reef that is ideal for snorkelling (see p19). You'll have to watch your step to get into the ocean, but once you're there you'll want to stay a while. This is the quintessential turquoise bay, with lush mountains behind and an island dominating the horizon.

BEWARE THE 4233

While Phuket is normally very safe, one stretch of Hwy 4233 has proven dangerous late at night. Over the past year at least four tourists have been pushed off their motorbikes on their way home from Kata to Rawai and then robbed at knifepoint. One Swedish tourist was murdered when he tried to fight back. If you're travelling by motorbike alone, and it's after midnight, the safe choice is to drive over Kata hill and link up with Hwy 402 to get back to Rawai. Ten extra minutes could be a life (or wallet) saver.

👁 LAEM PHROMTHEP

Hwy 4233; admission free

If you want to see the luscious Andaman Sea bend around Phuket, then you come here, to the island's southernmost point. Crowned by a mod lighthouse shaped like a concrete crab, and an evocative elephant shrine, you'll stay a while. At sunset the hordes descend in luxury buses, so if you crave privacy, take the faint fishermen's trail downhill to the rocky peninsula that reaches into the ocean and watch the sun drop in peace. For more information, see p22.

👁 RED GALLERY

☎ 087 8903722; www.phuketredgallery .com; 28/40 Moo 1, Th Sai Yuan; admission free; ⏲ 10am-7pm

Another of the area's fabulously funky artist-owned galleries. There are several artists showing here, but the star is Anda. She started by painting on wood and moved into inlays and other multimedia. Her work blends sculpture and painting.

◎ ROMADON GALLERY
☎ 087 2769507; 63/6 Th Sai Yuan; admission free; ⌚ appointment only
Surrealism lives on in the anthropomorphised animals gleaming on Romadan's canvases. He's painted here since 1975, and originality is the keyword. Our favourite was the canvas of night-blooming flowers, a Muslim crescent moon, leaf-shaped clouds and a spaceship. His

version of Pan, the human-goat God, is also unique. The doors are always open, but if you want to buy something, call the man.

◎ SECRET VIEW POINT
Hwy 4233; admission free
If you veer up the rise on the left instead of following the road to its end at Hat Nai Han, you will remain on Hwy 4233 towards Laem Phromthep. But you don't have to go that far for a sensational view. At the top of the hill there is a turn-off and a small gazebo to the right. Pull over here – you'll see a vendor and a few tourists, and you'll have an outrageous north-facing panorama sans tour buses.

Boats and beach, sea and sunset – picture-perfect Laem Phromthep

BEACHES & TOWNS

RAWAI

WAT CHALONG
Hwy 4021, Chalong; admission by donation; ⏰ 6am-6pm
This bustling, tiered temple has 36 Buddhas seated, reclining and meditating on the first two floors. Concrete serpents line the banisters and the lotus pond outside. It's not an antique, but it possesses a spiritual vibration, especially when worshippers pay their respects.

WAT NAI HAN
Hat Nai Han; admission free
During research, a new temple was under construction at this monastery compound. But it isn't the architecture that's interesting. This is a working monastery, so if you show up at dawn you can watch, or even join in, as the monks chant scripture. There are worse ways to begin a day. Ask permission from a monk the day before.

DO

ATSUMI HEALING *Spa*
☎ 081 2720571; www.atsumihealing .com; 34/18 Soi Pattana; spa treatments from 1000B
Atsumi isn't just a spa, it's an earthy fasting and detox retreat centre. Most guests come to fast on water, juice and/or herbs for days at a time. Massages are part of the programme, and the regularly eating public is welcome to book massages here. In addition

to traditional Thai, oil and deep-tissue treatments, you can get the signature ThaiAtsu massage (think Thai meets shiatsu). Meditative and gentle yoga classes with a touch of t'ai chi are also available.

BOAT CHARTERS
Watersports
Th Viset, Hat Rawai
Rawai is the best place to charter a boat to the neighbouring islands. You can lounge on nearby Ko Bon (800/2000B long tail/speedboat), snorkel off Coral island (1200/3000B) or Ko Racha (3000/7000B), and explore Ko Kai (4000/8000B). You can even charter a speedboat to Ko Phi-Phi (16,000B, 1½ hours) if public boating isn't your thing. There are several captains along the waterfront.

HERBAL STEAM SAUNA *Spa*
Th Viset; sauna/massage 100/250B; ⏰ 10am-9pm
Easily the best of the grassroots massage options, it has a wood-fired herbal sauna that will suck the toxins from your body and soul. And the massages, on thatched platforms, are equally blissful.

OFFSPRAY LEISURE
Watersports
☎ 081 8941274; www.offsprayleisure .com; 43/87 Chalong Plaza; trips 5 days per week from 2950B

Pricha 'Tuk' Chokkuea
Muay thai boxer and owner of Rawai Muay Thai

How did you get into boxing? We were very poor. I had no shoes. We lived in a house with a dirt floor, and for many poor Thai people boxing is seen as a way out. So when I was nine I begin training with my uncle. And when I was 10 I had my first fight. **How many fights have you had?** One hundred and sixty. And I've won 80% of them, including one championship belt. I won that in Patong stadium. **Was that your most memorable fight?** No. When I was 18, I fought in Bangkok's Lumpini Stadium. That's the top stadium in Thailand. There were 3000 people there. My purse was 45,000B. **Do you still plan to fight?** Now, I am a trainer. We train tourists (at Rawai Muay Thai) and that allows us to also train 10 to 15 good Thai fighters. They live at the gym for free, and we cover their expenses. That's *muay thai* tradition.

This dive and snorkelling excursion company specialises in trips to the reefs around Ko Phi-Phi. Its high-speed boat will get you there in 45 minutes, compared to the usual 1½ hours (minimum), which leaves you more time to enjoy the water. It also keeps its client loads small, which lends an intimate feel – something missing among most other dive operators in Phuket.

✈ PHUKET ELEPHANT RIDE
Animal Interaction
☎ 084 0583276; 25/19 Moo 1, Hwy 4233; elephant tours from 800B, snake show 400B, monkey show 400B; ⏰ 9am-7pm

If you can't be bothered driving the extra few kilometres to the superior Kok Chang Safari (p76), you can book a similar trip at Phuket Elephant Ride. Tours last 20, 30 or 60 minutes. The camp also features a snake show starring a king cobra and another somewhat depressing show with a trained monkey.

✈ PHUKET PARADISE 4WD TOUR *Adventure/Sports*
☎ 076 288501; 24/1 Moo 1, Hwy 4233; tours from 1500B; ⏰ 8.30am-6pm
As passenger or driver, you can 4WD on dirt roads through the jungles of Phuket. Tours last either one or two hours.

MUAY THAI

Muay thai (Thai Boxing) is both Thailand's indigenous martial art and the nation's favourite sport. Fall into any café or bar in the middle of the day and you're likely to see a *muay thai* bout on TV. What captivates is its emphasis on close-quarters fighting. Fighters use their knees, elbows, feet and fists to inflict damage.

And like any good martial art, *muay thai* has a helluva legend behind it. In 1774, when Myanmar (Burma) briefly ruled Thailand, the impulsive Burmese king held a seven-day, seven-night religious festival in honour of Lord Buddha. Overcome with a very un-Buddhist impulse, he wanted to see some blood during the festivities. So he called upon Nai Khanom Tom, a Thai prisoner of war and a *muay thai* expert, to fight a Burmese swordsman.

Nai Khanom Tom did a traditional Wai Kru pre-fight dance, which loosens up the fighter and honours the teacher, and in this case, the Burmese king. He then crushed his opponent. Baffled, the king made him fight another Burmese champion, and another. All told, Tom fought and defeated nine fighters in a row. He won his freedom (and two Burmese wives) that night.

Originally *muay thai* was taught in the military, but the Buddhist monasteries inherited stewardship, which helps explain why even today's fighters live like monks. They stay in gym dormitories and forsake alcohol and sex when in training. Sometimes their trainers institute a curfew, quite literally under lock and key. But fighters persevere because many of them come from extreme poverty and in Thailand *muay thai* is seen as a path to a better life.

🏇 PHUKET RIDING SCHOOL
Sports

☎ 076 288213; www.phuketridingclub
.com; 95 Th Vises; rides from 650B;
🕑 7am-6.30pm

Ride the jungle trails and white
sands of the south coast atop
Australian horses. The stables,
gear and horses are all top quality.
Lessons are also available.

🏇 RAWAI MUAY THAI *Sports*

☎ 081 0788067; www.rawaimuaythai
.com; 43/42 Moo 7, Th Sai Yuan;
group class 500B, private session 800B;
🕑 7.30-9.30am & 4-6pm

A former *muay thai* champion
opened this gym, and tourists
from around the world come here
to learn how to fight alongside
professional Thai fighters. Most
are college kids who live in on-site
dorms, but you're welcome to
drop in for lessons. Be warned. It's
immediately addictive.

🛍 SHOP
🛍 BZENTER *Design, Beauty*

Th Viset; 🕑 3pm-late

Here you'll find fantastic outdoor
art installations, a gorgeous
Ganesha shrine, the superb Vichen
Gallery – with fine modern sculpture and canvasses, a beauty salon,
Arlecchino's outrageous ice cream,
the Sirocco Bar and Da Vinci piz-
zeria, all in a mod, concrete art mall.

🍴 EAT
🍴 ARLECCHINO HOMEMADE ICE CREAM *Ice Cream* $

☎ 084 1040741; 8/46 Moo 1, Th Viset;
🕑 3-10pm; 🚹 🚻

It serves the greatest ice cream in
Phuket (certainly), Thailand (it has
to be), Asia (very probably), the
world (quite possibly). So unless
you hate sweet mango, tangy passionfruit and the richest, darkest
chocolate you could imagine, get
your ass over here.

🍴 BAAN RIMLAY *Thai* $$

Th Viset, Hat Rawai; 🕑 11am-11pm

The Thai seafood house to the
right of the pier steams clams,
mussels and fish, and grills squid,
prawns and lobster to perfection.
It also makes terrific soups and
salads if you'd rather eat light.
The seafood is a bit pricier here
than at the more humble seafood
joints down the street, but the
location is superb and the views
exceptional.

🍴 BLEU BLANC GRILL
French $$$

☎ 089 5947195; 7-/14 Moo 5, Th Viset;
🕑 6-11pm, closed Wed

The area's hot, new French
restaurant feels like a tented living
room, with sofas for booths and
a very chic blue décor. The grilled
meats (chicken, lamb and steak)

BEACHES & TOWNS

RAWAI

are superb. The exceptional caesar salad, with hard-boiled eggs, bacon and grilled chicken strips, is a meal in itself. And there's dinner music.

🍴 CHALONG NIGHT MARKET
Thai $
Hwy 402, just north of Chalong Circle; 🕑 **6-11pm Wed;** 🚹
One of the most popular night markets on the island. Vendors, farmers and local chefs converge under the gas lamps. Bring an appetite (that pumpkin curry looks good) and a shopping bag – it's always nice to have a mango in the morning.

🍴 CHAO KHUN
Thai, European $$
☎ **078 889032; 39/23 Th Viset;** 🕑 **8am-10pm**
Come to this charming corner café not for the dangling vines, leather chairs and red tablecloths, but for the all-you-can-eat breakfast buffet. It has everything from pancakes and French toast to made-to-order eggs, and beans and mushies.

🍴 DA VINCI *Italian* $$
☎ **076 289574; www.bzenter.com; 28/46 Moo 1, Th Viset;** 🕑 **5.30-10.30pm, closed Wed;** 🚹 Ⓥ
This authentic Italian kitchen is one of the best restaurants in the area. The staff is lovely and warm, the pizza wood fired, the dining room

stylish, the patio casual and artsy. The house wines rock too.

🍴 DON'S CAFÉ
Thai, American $$
☎ **076 289314; www.phuket-dons.com; Moo 7, 48/5 Th Sai Yuan;** 🕑 **8.30am-10.30pm;** 💻
This was the first restaurant geared to tourists in the area. It remains a hub of the local expat community, and it has terrific breakfasts and a lovely mango chicken dish.

🍴 GERMAN BAKERY
European $
☎ **084 8433288; Th Viset;** 🕑 **7.30am-6pm;** 🚹
</br>

TALAAT NAT
Rotating street markets *(talaat nat)* are popular in Phuket. Held at night under gas lamps, and often next to major highways or streets, they are essentially a series of stalls selling everything from fresh produce to thongs (flip-flops) to local sweets to some tremendously delicious, and cheap, street food – think grilled catfish, noodle and soup dishes, curries, *pàt tai* (Thai fried noodles, usually with peanuts) and fried chicken. The largest and most popular one happens on Wednesday night just north of Chalong Circle. Expats patronise them and tourists wander in now and then, but it's mainly a local Thai scene, where the working class gather, chat and have a nice dinner out under the stars.

Grocery shopping Thai-style

of white meat. So what if it still has Christmas streamers up in March?

🍴 LA CHAUMIERE
French, Thai $$

☎ 084 8452800; 50/7 Moo 7, Th Sai Yuan; ⏱ noon-10pm

This quaint, thatched dining room serves fish and beef in French or Thai style. Crab quiche and duck breast with apples are two of its more popular dishes.

🍴 LOBSTER RESTAURANT
Thai $

Hat Nai Han; ⏱ 10am-8pm

A lazy barefoot lunch on Hat Nai Han is sweet. You'll sit in bamboo chairs, listen to the birds and crashing waves, and order fresh seafood.

🍴 RAWAI NIGHT MARKET
Thai $

Hwy 402; ⏱ 6-11pm Tue & Thu; 🚼

Similar to but much smaller than the Chalong Night Market, this market is patronised almost exclusively by Rawai locals.

🍴 RAWAI SEAFOOD GRILLS
Thai $

Th Viset, Hat Rawai; ⏱ 11am-10pm

There are dozens of grill huts on Rawai's beach road, and it doesn't much matter which one you choose. All the fish is fresh; the clams, mussels, prawns and lobster are not to be overlooked

This friendly and fun restaurant run by a German-Thai couple has the best pastries in the area. It also makes a fine brown bread, serves delicious breakfasts, and has amazing bratwurst and sauerkraut. The food is simple, but always very good.

🍴 KITCHEN GRILL *Thai* $

☎ 081 0770853; Th Viset; ⏱ 8am-10pm

The stodgy brick décor doesn't do this tidy, tasty kitchen justice. Kitchen Grill has speciality produce, such as radicchio, that even some of the big resorts don't have. And its searing green curry with chicken has large, tender chunks either. Make sure you try the spicy sauce, not that sweet and sour syrup. The prices are so good you will be stunned. And like the Governator, you will be back. For more information, see p18.

🍴 ROTI HOUSE *Thai* $
☎ 083 10762761; 81/6 Soi Samekka; ⏱ 5-11am; ♿

If you like French toast or croissants in the morning, you'll love roti, Thailand's Muslim morning delicacy. You'll receive a plate of savoury crepes and a bowl of sweet breakfast curry, then dunk, eat, repeat. This is a local hang-out and you will be welcomed with warm smiles.

🍴 RUM JUNGLE
Mediterranean $$
☎ 076 388153; 69/8 Th Sai Yuan; ⏱ 5-11pm, closed Sun

The best restaurant in the area, with a Mediterranean kitchen run by a terrific Aussie chef. The thatched dining room is patrolled by a fun Thai crew, and the food is dynamite. Who knew penne and meatballs or fish and chips could be this fine? The Argentinean tenderloin is also divine, and so is the world-beat soundtrack.

🍴 SOM TUM LANNA *Thai*
☎ 086 5932711; 2/16 Th Sai Yuan; ⏱ 8am-5pm, closed Mon

Booze on wheels – VW Bar

This place has three dishes worth mentioning: the salted, grilled red snapper; the grilled chicken; and the paint-peelingly spicy *som tum* (green papaya salad). Now, the fish is very good, but you can find its equal on Hat Rawai. The chicken on the other hand…well, heed the words of another blissed-out, greasy-mouthed customer: 'This is some fucking killer fucking chicken!' As for the *som tum*? Don't be a hero. Order it mild. It will still bring some serious heat.

DRINK

COFFEE@HOME *Café*
☎ 076 388608; 97/21 Th Sai Yuan;
⏱ 9am-10pm; 🖥
The coffee is good, and the internet connection is decent. You can also scan, fax and copy.

FREEDOM PUB *Pub*
☎ 076 287402; Th Viset, Hat Rawai;
⏱ 3pm-2am
Upon first glance it looks like a typical bar-girl haunt, but it really is a terrific tropical dive bar that men and women will enjoy. The staff is friendly, a bar is inside and a wonderful circle bar outside, and it has live music most nights.

NIKITA'S *Café, Bar*
☎ 076 288703; Th Viset, Hat Rawai;
⏱ noon-midnight

Nikita's is a pleasant place to hang, with coffee drinks, green teas, a nice selection of shakes and furniture carved from driftwood. The bamboo bar has good whiskey, and if you're hungry, you can order from Baan Rimlay next door. So what if the Thai waitresses say, 'oy', to get your attention? Blame it on the Royal Navy.

THE ROYAL PHUKET YACHT CLUB *Hotel, Bar*
☎ 076 380200; www.theroyalphuket yachtclub.com; 23/3 Moo 1;
⏱ 9am-midnight
Formerly the Royal Meridian Yacht Club, this once-great resort is the reason for all the yachts in the bay. Time has left their mark on these old bones, but that patio bar… Wow! From here there is nothing but turquoise sea and island views. It's a location that demands a beverage. And another one after that.

VW BAR *Bar*
Th Viset; ⏱ 5pm-midnight, closed on rainy days
When a mint-condition, retro-fitted, VW bus parks in a vacant lot, you notice. When the attractive driver/barkeep subsequently opens the roof up to reveal a full wet bar and sets up tables and chairs beneath the stars, you pull over and order a drink.

>HAT KAMALA & HAT SURIN

North of Patong the pace of both tourism, and life, mellows. And with gorgeous turquoise bays like these to marvel at, it's a wonder anything gets done. What does pass for work in these parts largely happens on the beach. Most restaurants and shops open for business on, or just steps from, the sand. Five-star Surin is more stylish and refined, and frankly is better looking than Kamala, its older, three-star, relentlessly barefoot cousin. But with new, luxe development projects underway on Kamala's cliffs, this scruffy, charming and very laid-back enclave may soon be forced into sophistication. For now, though, it's still the kind of place where you could go a week without having to wear a shirt.

HAT KAMALA & HAT SURIN

👁 SEE
Masjid Mukaram Bang Tao	**1**	C2
Phuket Fantasea	**2**	C6

🏃 DO
Amanpuri Spa	**3**	A1
Beach House Cooking School	**4**	B3
Jet-Ski Hire	**5**	B3
Kamala Dive Center	**6**	C5
Kamala Diving Center	**7**	B6
Longtail Charters	**8**	B6
Palm Spa	**9**	B2
Parasailing	(see 5)	
Scuba Quest	**10**	C6

🛍 SHOP
Heritage Collection	**11**	B3
Soul of Asia	(see 12)	
Surin Plaza	**12**	C2

🍽 EAT
Basilico	**13**	B6
Carmen	**14**	B2
Deng's	**15**	C5
La Plage	**16**	B3
Ma Ma Fati Ma	**17**	C4
Nanork Seafood	**18**	C5
Patcharin Seafood	**19**	B3
Paula's Cafe Retro	**20**	B3
Pla Seafood	**21**	B3
Positano's	**22**	B3

Rockfish	**23**	B6
Silk	**24**	C2
The Catch	**25**	B2
Weaves	**26**	B2

🍸 DRINK
Liquid Lounge	**27**	B3
Taste	(see 21)	

⭐ PLAY
The Catch Beach Club	(see 25)	

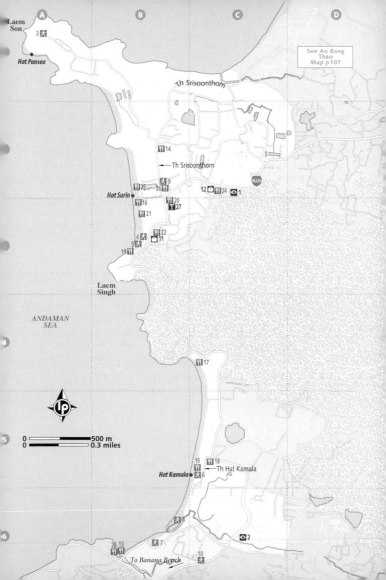

A

Laem
Son

3 ⚑

Hat Pansea ●

B

C

See Ao Bang
Thao
Map p107

D

Th Srisoonthorn

🍴 14

← Th Srisoonthorn

🍴 25 ⚑ 9
26 🍴

4025

Hat Surin ●

12 ⧉ 24 ⚑ 1

🍴 16
🍴 21

🍴 20
🍴 27

4 ⚑
5

22 🍴
11 ⧉

19 🍴

Laem
Singh

ANDAMAN
SEA

🍴 17

⬆
LP

0 ━━━━━━ 500 m
0 ━━━━━━ 0.3 miles

15 🍴 18
🍴

Hat Kamala ●   ⚑ 6   ← Th Hat Kamala

⚑ 2

⚑ 8

28 13   ⚑ 7
🍴🍴

To Banana Beach

10
⚑

HAT KAMALA

A chilled-out hybrid of Hat Karon and Hat Surin, calm but fun Kamala tends to lure a mixture of longer-term guests (some of whom appear to suffer from adult-onset adolescence), a regular crop of Scandinavian families and young couples. The bay is magnificent, turquoise and serene with shore breakers that lull you to sleep. Palms and pines mingle on the leafy and rocky northern end where the water is a rich emerald. The snorkelling around the rock reef is entrancing, while new resorts are ploughed into the southern bluffs above the gathering long tails. The entire beach is backed with rolling, palm-draped hills, which one can only hope the developers leave alone. Forever. And it's also the only beach with a walking path lined with restaurants, resorts and shops. So ditch the motorbike and step into Kamala bliss.

SEE

PHUKET FANTASEA

☎ 076 385000; www.phuket-fantasea .com; 99 Moo 3, Th Hat Kamela; admission with/without dinner 1900/1500B; 🕑 6-11.30pm Fri-Wed
Interested in a US$60 million 'cultural theme park' located just north of Hat Kamala? This ain't Disneyland, but there is a show that takes the colour and pageantry of traditional Thai dance and combines them with Vegas-style production value (think 30 elephants). All of this takes place on a stage dominated by a full-scale replica of a Khmer temple reminiscent of Angkor Wat. Kids may be captivated but it's over-the-top cheesy. Tickets can be booked through most hotels and tour agencies. No cameras allowed.

DO

KAMALA DIVE CENTER
Watersports
☎ 076 385254; www.kamaladivecenter .com; 95/2 Moo 3, Th Hat Kamala; dive trips from 2200B; 🕑 9am-9pm
An intimate, family-run dive centre, this place can book you on trips to the popular reefs southeast of Phuket, but it also offers shorter, and very reasonably priced, trips to the pristine beaches and coves of deserted Banana Rock and its beach. It teaches the full array of courses as well.

KAMALA DIVING CENTER
Watersports
☎ 076 385518; 74/3 Moo 3, Th Hat Kamala; day trips from 2500B
New to Kamala, and also known as Merlin Diving, this diving

Khun Job
Lead Singer of Job To Do

How long have you lived in Phuket? Almost 30 years. I first came here when I was 21. **What has been the biggest change?** Plastic! Before in Thailand we eat on banana leaf and after you can throw it anywhere. Now many people are doing the same thing with plastic. **Your favourite beach?** Nai Han, and I also like Nai Yang very much. But I lived in Kamala for long time. **Your favourite island?** Ko Yao. **Do you have a favourite restaurant?** I like to eat at the markets. You can find organic food there. We are not true Rasta, but we follow the natural way. Now in Phuket is getting more difficult to live with nature. People start building everywhere, but we still must try. **What do you like to eat there?** Nam Prik. It's shrimp paste. That's what I grew up with. For me, it's like medicine.

centre offers trips to Banana Rock Beach, as well as long day trips to the Similan Islands.

🚣 LONGTAIL CHARTERS
Watersports
South Hat Kamala; per day from 3500B
Long tails are available to nearby Banana Rock Beach and to Freedom Beach south of Patong.

🚣 SCUBA QUEST *Watersports*
☎ 076 279016; www.scuba-quest
-phuket.com; 93/13 Moo 3, Th Hat
Kamala; day trips from 2200B
Local dives are accessed from a long-tail boat, and it has longer day trips to the common Phuket dive haunts.

🍴 EAT

🍴 BASILICO *Italian* $$
☎ 076 385856; 125 Moo 3, Th Hat
Kamala; 🕐 6-11pm; **V**
Another member of Phuket's ever-growing legion of tasty Italian restaurants. It has good wood-fired pizza, but try the grilled tiger prawns in a parsley and garlic marinade, served on a chickpea and rosemary mash.

🍴 DENG'S *Thai, European* $
☎ 076 385981; Soi Police Station;
🕐 8am-11pm; ♿
The best meal on this end of the beach. You can get your pasta,

burgers and Wiener schnitzel here, but you'd be better served by the pineapple fried rice or local seafood.

🍴 MA MA FATI MA
Thai $
far north end of Hat Kamala; ♿
This beachfront snack shack is a real find. The family who owns and operates it could not be more welcoming. The tasty Thai food is exceptional and so are the fresh fruit shakes. And if you forget your wallet, they'll still feed you and trust that you'll pay later. Try that in the Western world.

🍴 NANORK SEAFOOD
Thai $$
☎ 076 279144; 94/19 Moo 3, Tambon
Kamala; 🕐 11am-10pm; ♿
A charming stone and timber seafood restaurant with a daily mixed-grill selection and blooming flowers on tables nestled in the sand.

🍴 ROCKFISH *Fusion* $$
☎ 076 279732; www.rockfish
restaurant.com; 33/6 Th Hat Kamala;
🕐 8am-late
Perched above the river mouth and the bobbing long tails, with beach, bay and mountain views, is Kamala's best dining room. Its eclectic brand of fusion won it Phuket's restaurant of the year in

2005, and it's still rolling out gems like its fried red crab, and seafood wontons wrapped in a rice crepe with apple, guava and cinnamon compote. And the 99B Bloody Mary doesn't suck either.

HAT SURIN

Like that hot boy or girl in school who also happens to have style, soul, a fun personality and wealthy parents, Surin is the kind of place that can inspire (travel) lust in anyone who encounters it. With its wide white-sand beach, water that blends from pale turquoise in the shallows to a deep blue on the horizon, and two lush, boulder-strewn headlands, Surin could easily attract tourists on its looks alone. Ah, but it has so much more to offer: there are stunning galleries, five-star spa resorts and wonderful beachfront dining options, too. So by the time you're done swimming, sunbathing, snacking at local fish grills and sipping cocktails at barefoot-chic beach clubs, don't be surprised if you've fallen hopelessly in love.

SEE
MASJID MUKARAM BANG TAO
Hwy 4025; admission free

The peeling, white façade and sea-green mosaic domes make for a striking image against the blue sky and jungled hills. Come at the obligatory hour and you'll glimpse a steady, serene stream of prayer traffic. Visitors are welcome.

DO
AMANPURI SPA *Spa*
☎ 076 324333; www.amanresorts.com; 118/1 Moo 3, Th Srisoonthorn; treatments from 3500B; 9am-9pm
Therapy commingles with luxury at this cliffside spa set in a secluded coconut grove. Treatment rooms are all wood and glass with private steam rooms and meditation gardens. The spa uses its own brand of all-natural, organic products and resort guests can wake up with an early-morning yoga class.

BEACH HOUSE COOKING SCHOOL *Cooking Classes*
☎ 089 6511064; Hat Surin; class per person 1900B; 9am-10pm
At this chic beach café you first peruse the menu, then circle the intriguing dishes, because you'll learn to make them during the three-hour cooking class run by the owner/chef. The dining room has live trees rising through the roof, and the student kitchen has ocean views.

Soak away your aches and pains in the spa (p101) at Amanpuri Resort

🏃 JET-SKI HIRE *Watersports*
Hat Surin; hire per 30min 1500B
Speed freaks can buzz the beautiful bay on a selection of well-maintained jet skis. Or hop on a banana raft and hold on tight as a speedboat whips you around the sea (500B).

🏃 PALM SPA *Spa*
☎ 076 316500; www.twinpalms
-phuket; 106/46 Moo 3, Th Srisoonthorn;
treatments from 2000B; ⏱ 9am-9pm
Pamper yourself with a yoghurt and coffee body scrub, coconut cream bath and/or a hot-stone massage at this luxury spa on the

main drag. It also has a full range of beauty services.

🏄 PARASAILING *Watersports*
Hat Surin; per trip 1500B
It feels good to fly, especially high above stunning Surin.

SHOP
📷 HERITAGE COLLECTION
Design, Homewares
☎ 076 271144; Th Hat Surin;
🕙 9am-9pm
Without a doubt, the owner of this gallery (he has two galleries in Phuket and another two in Bangkok) has the single best collection of traditional Southeast Asian art in Thailand. In this museum-quality showroom there are 3m Buddhas encrusted with precious stones, ancient teak shrines, Buddha's glorious footprint carved from sandstone and a large alabaster Buddha carved from one rock. Some pieces are for sale (deals are only done face to face and prices can be more than one million baht). Others are just for show.

📷 SOUL OF ASIA
Design, Homewares
☎ 076 211122; Surin Plaza, 5/50 Moo 3, Hwy 4025; 🕙 10.30am-8pm
A lovely gallery filled with both funky and fine Southeast Asian modern art, Soul of Asia also has

a few antiques and traditional pieces mixed in.

📷 SURIN PLAZA
Fashion, Design
☎ 076 271241; 5/50 Moo 3, Hwy 4025;
🕙 10am-10pm
This stylish shopping mall just a short jaunt from the beach is filled with chic clothing boutiques and art galleries.

EAT
🍴 CARMEN *Thai, Italian* $$
☎ 076 325713; 14/1 Moo 3, Th Hat Surin;
🕙 11am-midnight
A sweet fusion spot with sponge-painted coral walls and peeling concrete floors. Order anything from steamed sea bass to homemade spinach ravioli.

🍴 LA PLAGE *Thai, French* $$
☎ 081 847719; Hat Surin;
🕙 11am-10pm; 👶
When two Laotian sisters, who were raised in Paris and speak four languages fluently, open a fusion restaurant on the sand, it's worth experiencing. They have a fine *nicoise* salad and a savoury green curry with a kick.

🍴 PATCHARIN SEAFOOD
Thai $
☎ 081 8928587; Hat Surin;
🕙 11am-10pm; 👶

Beginning with Patacharin, a local fish grill built into the headland at the southernmost end of Hat Surin, fish grills and cafés unfurl north like a strand of delicious pearls.

🍽 PAULA'S CAFÉ RETRO
American $$
☎ 076 270283; 106/41 Moo 3, Th Hat Surin; 🕙 8am-5pm; ♿
You'll go to Paula's for bagels and cream cheese, homemade yoghurt and breakfast burritos in the morning, and BLT's, *quesadillas* and quiche in the afternoon.

🍽 PLA SEAFOOD
Austrian, Thai $$
☎ 076 325572; Hat Surin; 🕙 11am-10pm
Pla delivers the unlikely pairing of Thai and Austrian cuisine, which means you can have your barbecued squid and steamed crab with Wiener schnitzel, amid stylish, beach environs.

🍽 POSITANO'S *Italian* $$
☎ 076 270597; 106/17 Moo 3, Th Hat Surin; 🕙 11.30am-2pm & 5.30-11pm
Choose between lobster linguini and 23 varieties of pizza at this authentic Italian restaurant.

🍽 SILK *Thai* $$$
☎ 076 271705; Hwy 4025; 🕙 11am-11pm

This expansive, stylish place is one of several upmarket restaurants in Surin Plaza, and is an expat magnet. The décor is a hip cocktail of burgundy paint, wood and exotic flowers, while the menu focuses on beautifully executed Thai specialities.

🍽 THE CATCH
Fusion $$$
☎ 076 316500; Hat Surin; 🕙 11am-11pm
Slip on your spaghetti-strapped dress or your linen suit to blend in at this cabana-style eatery right on the beach. It's part of Twin Palms and has the same classy attributes as the hotel, offering both ambiance and cuisine, plus a salsa soundtrack.

🍽 WEAVES
Fusion $$$
☎ 076 270900; 121/1 Th Srisoonthorn; 🕙 5-11pm
Set in a gorgeous atrium with flowing fountains, a lotus pond and old timber floors is this appetising fusion restaurant attached to the Manathai resort. Its idea of surf and turf is steamed monkfish and osso bucco.

🍸 DRINK
🍸 LIQUID LOUNGE *Lounge*
☎ 081 5372018; Th Hat Surin; 🕙 4pm-1am; 🖥

A stylish, loft-style martini lounge with premium liquor, occasional live jazz and wi-fi.

ⓨ TASTE *Tapas Bar*
☎ 087 8866401; www.tastesurinbeach.com; Hat Surin; ⏰ 4-11pm
The hopelessly hip, concrete-slab interior is softened by the orchids and the sound of the sea. Happy hour, with 99B tapas and cocktails, lasts from 4pm to 7pm.

⭐ PLAY
⭐ THE CATCH BEACH CLUB
Music Venue
☎ 076 316500; Hat Surin; admission free; ⏰ 11am-1am
This gorgeous lounge attached to the restaurant attracts live international artists for extended runs, and reminds us that there are few things in life that can trump good live music on the beach.

>AO BANG THAO

Almost as large and even more beautiful than Ao Patong, the stunning, 8km white-sand sweep of Ao Bang Thao is the glue that binds the region's disparate elements. The southern half is home to a sprinkling of three-star bungalow resorts and cafés. Further inland you'll find an old fishing village laced with canals along with a number of upstart villa subdivisions. Don't be alarmed if you see a herd of water buffalo grazing just 100m from a gigantic construction site. That's how fast Bang Thao is changing.

Smack in the centre of it all is the somewhat absurd Laguna Phuket complex – a network of five-star resorts and an aging shopping mall knitted together by a man-made lake, patrolled by tourist shuttle boats, and a paved nature trail. Not so magical. But in the north, mother nature asserts herself once more, as a lonely stretch of powder-white sand and tropical blue extends past all the bustle and change and delivers the kind of peace you imagined when you booked your trip.

AO BANG THAO

🏃 DO
Bangthao Beach Riding
  Club 1 D4
Hideaway Day Spa 2 D4
Pearl Andaman Diving ... 3 B5

🍴 EAT
Babylon Beach Club 4 B4
Cafe Java 5 B4
Rain-Hail 6 B4
Royal Indian Food 7 B5
Tatonka 8 D4
Tawai Restaurant 9 D5
Tik Restaurant 10 B4

🍸 DRINK
English Pub 11 B2
Reggae Bar 12 B4

⭐ PLAY
Jackie O's 13 D5

A
B
C
D

Laguna Phuket

11 ⛲

Laguna Phuket

Canal Health Clinic •

Th Laguna

Ao Bang Thao

Laguna Phuket

Th Laguna **1**

12 ⛲
10 🍴
4 🍴

6 🍴

CHOENG THALEH

2 🏊
Th Srisoonthorn **8** 🍴

9 🍴 **13** ⭐ • **Police**

Hat Bang Thao •

4030

5 🍴

7 🍴

3 🏊

Th Hat Bang Thao

CHOENG THALEH

See Hat Kamala & Hat Surin Map p97

0   1 km
0   0.6 miles

BEACHES & TOWNS

AO BANG THAO

🏃 DO

🏃 BANGTHAO BEACH RIDING CLUB *Sports*

☎ 076 324199; 394 Moo 1, Th Hat Bang Thao; horseback rides from 1000B, elephant rides from 350B

Aptly named, this riding club offers everything from 10-minute elephant rides to half-day horseback rides through forest and marsh and along virgin beach, to serious riding lessons. The club is located near the Laguna Phuket entrance.

🏃 HIDEAWAY DAY SPA *Spa*

☎ 076 271549; Th Laguna; treatments from 1500B; ⏱ 9am-9pm

One of Phuket's first spas, Hideaway offers traditional Thai massage, sauna and mud body wraps in a tranquil wooded setting at the edge of a lagoon.

🏃 PEARL ANDAMAN DIVING *Watersports*

☎ 076 270536; www.pearlandaman .com; 82/16 Moo 3, Th Hat Bang Thao, Choeng Thaleh; dive trips from 3500B

Enjoy the crisp modern lines and the Pacific Rim cuisine at Rain-Hail

A solid outfitter that leads day trips to the local reefs around Ko Waeo and to the Similan Islands.

⊗ EAT

⊗ BABYLON BEACH CLUB
Thai $$

☎ 081 9705302; www.babylonbeach club.com; Hat Bang Thao;
🕑 10am-11pm; ♿

Accessible by dirt road are the polished, whitewashed tiki environs of the Babylon Beach Club. The food is nice, and all the Thai specialities are on offer, along with fresh grilled seafood and good burgers. Dishes are served on banana leaf liners, and four tables are set up with white tablecloths and umbrellas mere centimetres from the sea.

⊗ CAFE JAVA
French, Thai $$

☎ 087 2668664; 73/3 Moo 3, Choeng Thaleh; 🕑 7.30am-11pm

Sample first-rate French and Thai food on a deck overlooking beautiful southern Hat Bang Thao. It has scrambled eggs with asparagus for breakfast and duck confit for dinner.

⊗ RAIN-HAIL
Fusion $$$

☎ 081 9791967; www.rain-hail.com; 21 Moo 2, Choeng Thaleh; 🕑 11.30am-2am

Not many miles to Babylon...Beach Club

Modernists will appreciate the black-bottom fountain in the entry, which juxtaposes a white-marble and limestone dining room on one side and a classic mod lounge on the other. The cuisine is all Pacific Rim, with a *tamago* roll of miso, mango and crab, and a lovely bluefin tuna tartare.

⊗ ROYAL INDIAN FOOD
Indian $

☎ 081 4154391; 69/12 Th Hat Bang Thao, Choeng Thaleh; 🕑 9am-10pm; V

Order all your subcontinental favourites from stuffed *parotha*

Seafood on the sand at Tik Restaurant

to *sag paneer* and chicken tikka. Delivery to your hotel is available for free.

🍴 TATONKA
Fusion $$$
☎ 076 324349; Th Srisoonthorn;
🕐 5-11pm Thu-Tue
Harold Schwarz developed his 'Globe Trotter' cuisine by taking fresh local products and combining them with cooking and presentation techniques learned in Europe, Colorado and Hawaii. The eclectic, tapas-style selec-

tion includes creative vegetarian and seafood dishes and such delights as Peking duck pizza (220B). There's also a tasting menu (750B per person, minimum two people), which lets you try a little of everything. Make reservations in the high season.

🍴 TAWAI RESTAURANT
Thai $$
☎ 076 325381; Moo 1, Laguna Phuket entrance; 🕐 6-11pm
Set in a lovely old house decorated with traditional art is this

gem of a Thai kitchen serving classics like roast duck curry and pork *larb* (minced chicken, beef or pork salad mixed with chilli, mint and coriander), and steamed, grilled and fried seafood.

 TIK RESTAURANT
Thai $$
☎ 089 4755053; 41/6 Moo 3, Hat Bang Thao; ⏱ 11am-10pm; 👶
Tik is among several local Thai restaurants on this stretch of beach specialising in fresh grilled seafood.

▼ DRINK

▼ ENGLISH PUB
Pub
☎ 089 8721398; Th Srisoonthorn, Hat Bang Thao; ⏱ noon-1am
Also known as 'The Whispering Cock', this timber-and-thatch watering hole is the most authentic English pub on the island – even the toilets smell. It has a sunny beer garden, a snug interior, a good range of beers and some decent pub grub.

▼ REGGAE BAR
Bar
Hat Bang Thao; ⏱ 11am-1am
If you have had your fill of cosy Babylon, stroll to this tiki bar, where you can kick back and let Bob Marley soothe your soul.

★ PLAY

 ★ JACKIE O
Bar, Music Venue
☎ 089 4740431; Moo 1, Laguna Phuket entrance; admission free; ⏱ 6pm-1am
A cosy circle bar with live rock and roll three nights a week and disco on Tuesday.

>THALANG & AROUND

There is life beyond the beach. Phuket's northeastern hemisphere, once a living breathing film set for *Good Morning Vietnam*, is laced with temples, waterfalls, singing gibbons, adrenaline-addled zip lines and some photogenic golf courses.

A drive to the Phuket Gibbon Rehabilitation Centre within the Khao Phra Thaew National Park will take you past most of the sites, and once you commune with the gibbons the rest are just a few minutes away. If you can, crown the day with a sunset meal on the floating dock at Bang Rong pier, where the fish is fresh, the sky blushes a deep pink and the call to prayer filters through the mangroves with a bittersweet whisper.

THALANG & AROUND

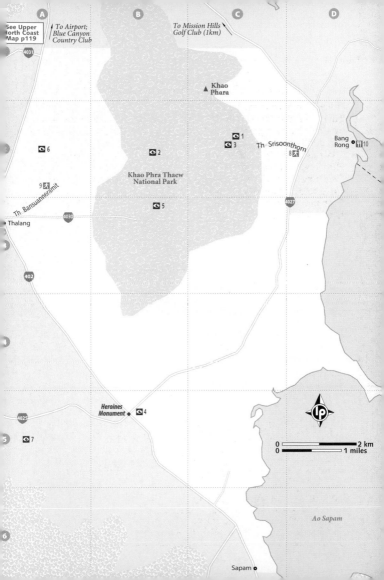

See Upper North Coast Map p119

A

B

C

D

4031

To Airport; Blue Canyon Country Club

To Mission Hills Golf Club (1km)

▲ Khao Phara

🕐 6

🕐 2

🕐 1

🕐 3

Th Srisoonthorn

8 🏊

Bang Rong

🍴 10

Khao Phra Thaew National Park

9 🏊

Th Bansuanneramit

4030

🕐 5

Thalang

4027

402

4025

Heroines Monument

🕐 4

🕐 7

Ao Sapam

0 ——————— 2 km
0 ——————— 1 miles

Sapam

👁 SEE

👁 BANG PAE FALLS

Khao Phra Thaew National Park, access from Hwy 4027; admission free
The waterfall is a 300m walk up a jungled earth and concrete path from the gibbon rehab centre, and you can hear the gibbons' haunting songs all the way. During the dry season, the waterfall isn't exactly spectacular, but there are swimming holes deep enough for daring jumps.

👁 KHAO PHRA THAEW NATIONAL PARK

☎ 076 311998; Hwy 4030, continue east at Heroine's monument; per person 200B
The last of Phuket's virgin rainforest is within the boundaries of this reserve, which includes the Phuket Gibbon Rehabilitation Centre (right) and two waterfalls. There once were tigers and Malayan sun bears here, but today it's a habitat island that still suffers from timber poaching. It isn't lifeless, however. There are monkeys, langur, civets, flying foxes, cobras and wild pigs in the bush, and there are some wild and semi-wild gibbon families thanks to rehab (see right). Khao Phra is the park's highest peak at 442m. There are guided 6km hikes available from Ton Sai falls (opposite) to Bang Pae falls. Guides gather at Ton Sai (the park's HQ)

Make an offering at Wat Phra Thong

in the morning and charge about 1000B for the day. This is the best way to experience the park.

👁 PHUKET GIBBON REHABILITATION CENTRE

☎ 076 260492; www.gibbonproject.org; donations encouraged; ☽ 9am-4pm
Housed within the Khao Phra Thaew National Park (left) near Bang Pae falls, this captivating centre adopts gibbons that have been kept (and often abused) in captivity and re-introduces them to the wild. A mere 1500B donation will care for a gibbon for a full year. For more information, see boxed text, opposite, and p16.

☉ THALANG NATIONAL MUSEUM

☎ **076 311426; cnr Hwy 4030 & Hwy 402; admission 30B;** ⏰ **8.30am-4pm**

The museum contains five exhibit halls chronicling Phuket's history and tracing the various ethnicities found in southern Thailand. The legend of the 'two heroines' (memorialised on the nearby monument), who supposedly drove off an 18th-century Burmese invasion force by convincing the island's women to dress like men, is also recounted in detail utilising backlit display panels and touch-screen electronic presentations. The prize artefact is a 2.3m-tall statue of Vishnu, which dates to the 9th century and was found in Takua Pa nearly 100 years ago.

☉ TON SAI FALLS

☎ **076 311998; Khao Phra Thaew National Park; admission free**

This waterfall will not be inducted into the natural splendour hall of fame. Certainly not during the trickling dry season, but the hike from here to Bang Pae is a good one. Get here early to find a guide.

☉ WAT PHRA THONG

Hwy 402; admission by donation; ⏰ **dawn-dusk**

Phuket's 'Temple of the Gold Buddha' is half buried so that only the head and shoulders are visible above ground. According to local legend, those who have tried to excavate the image have become very ill or encountered serious accidents. The temple is particularly revered by Thai Chinese, many of whom believe the image hails from China. During Chinese New Year pilgrims descend from Phang-Nga, Takua Pa and Krabi. In addition to Phra Thong there are 11 other Buddha images, including a Phra Praket

PLEASE DON'T CALL US MONKEYS

White Handed Gibbons (*Hylobates lar*) are apes. Which means they are much higher on the evolutionary scale than mere monkeys, and share some human characteristics. The most obvious is their four fingers and opposable thumb, matched by their four toes with an opposable big toe. Sound familiar? They use these humanlike digits to climb and swing from tree to tree at high speeds. They also have very similar senses to ours, including colour vision. They mate for life (they live between 30 and 40 years) and nest as a family unit as well. But they're arboreal, which means they spend their lives in trees as opposed to suburbs. Which is why they are endangered. As the Southeast Asian rainforests continue to fall, gibbon populations will continue to dwindle towards extinction.

(an unusual pose in which the Buddha is touching his own head with his right hand). Each promises a different virtue (success, health, wealth etc) to those who make offerings.

WAT THEP WANARAM
**Hwy 4025; admission by donation;
⏲ dawn-dusk**
Often ignored by tourists, this monastery and temple compound is suffused with incense, and rings with the sound of chanting monks in the morning. Check out the shrine to their founder.

🏃 DO
🏃 BANG PAE SAFARI
Adventure, Sports
**☎ 076 311163; 12/3 Moo 5, Th Srisoonthorn; tours from 800B;
⏲ 7.30am-5pm**
Based on the outskirts of the Khao Phra Thaew National Park (p114), this elephant trek, 4WD and canoe outfitter brings guests through the nearby rubber plantations and canals. The tour is fairly soft as far as adventure goes, and is best done in the wet season.

Speed from cliff to tree on the zip lines at Cable Jungle Adventure

BEACHES & TOWNS

THALANG & AROUND

⚐ BLUE CANYON COUNTRY CLUB *Sports*
☎ 076 328088; www.bluecanyonclub.com; 165 Moo 1, Th Thepkasattri; 18 holes 5300B

A luxury country club with two championship golf courses that have hosted two dramatic (and one record setting) Tiger Woods tournament wins. There is also a full-service spa, two restaurants and luxury apartments on the property. The facilities are showing their age, but you'll come for the golf course. It's a good one. Club hire and lessons are available.

⚐ CABLE JUNGLE ADVENTURE *Adventure, Sports*
☎ 081 9774904; 232/17 Moo 8, Th Bansuanneramit; per person 1600B; ⌚ 9am-6pm

In the hills behind a quilt of pineapple fields, rubber plantations and mango groves is this maze of eight zip lines linking cliffs to ancient ficus trees. The zips range from 6m to 23m above the ground and the longest run is 100m long. Closed-toe shoes are a must.

⚐ MISSION HILLS GOLF CLUB *Sports*
☎ 076 310888; www.missionhillsphuket.com; 195 Moo 4, Pla Khlok; 18 holes 3800B

Another 27 holes of tournament-calibre golf can be found at this Jack Nicklaus–designed course near the east coast. It, too, has a spa and hotel rooms and two swimming pools.

🍴 EAT
🍴 BANG RONG SEAFOOD *Thai*
Bang Rong pier; ⌚ 10am-9pm

This fish-farm-turned-restaurant is set on a floating pier in the luscious mangroves. It has red and white snapper, crab and mussels, and it plucks your catch after you order, so you know it's fresh. You can have it steamed, fried or grilled, but it's a Muslim enterprise so you can't have beer. Come at sunset, when fishermen chat on the dock, and the light plays on both the water and the mangroves. It's a special scene.

>UPPER NORTH COAST

Just minutes from the airport are some of the best and least developed beaches in Phuket. Hat Mai Khao, a 17km beach that was for years the sole domain of the JW Marriott Phuket Resort & Spa, fishermen and sea turtles (they lay their eggs here), now shares space with a few beach bungalow properties and the new, stylish Sala Resort. Hat Nai Yang and Hat Nai Thon are small barefoot resort areas where, thankfully, there isn't much to do but snorkel, dive, surf (with or without kites), sunbathe and eat grilled fish. Sirinat National Park preserves an 8km beach and the green hills behind it. And Yacht Haven Phuket Marina, on the northern-most tip, lives up to its name. So if you're looking to charter a sailboat or make like a San Tropez billionaire, you'll come here.

UPPER NORTH COAST

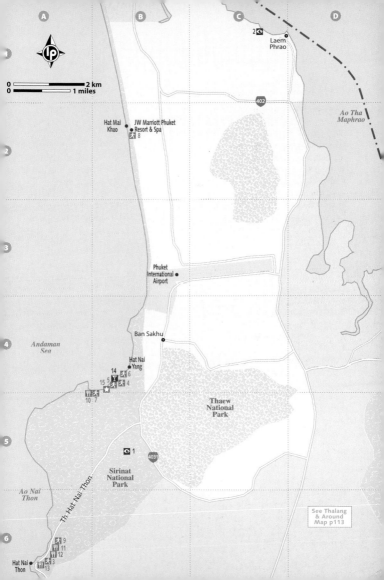

A
B
C
D

1

2 km
1 miles

2

Hat Mai
Khao

JW Marriott Phuket
Resort & Spa
8

402

Ao Tha
Maphrao

Laem
Phrao

2

3

Phuket
International
Airport

4

Andaman
Sea

Ban Sakhu

Hat Nai
Yang

14
15 5 6
10 7 4

Thaew
National
Park

5

Sirinat
National
Park

1
4031

Ao Nai
Thon

Th Hat Nai Thon

See Thalang
& Around
Map p113

6

Hat Nai Thon

9
11
12
3
13

HAT NAI THON

If you're after a lovely arc of fine golden sand, far from the buzz of Phuket busyness, Nai Thon is your Eden. It's accessed by a sinuous road through rubber plantations and banana groves. All you'll see here is a quiet main strip, a cosy turquoise bay and a few long tails bobbing back to the fish market on nearby Hat Nai Yang.

🏃 DO

🤿 AQUA DIVERS *Watersports*
☎ 076 205440; **www.aquadives.com**; **23/26 Th Hat Nai Thon; dives from 1590B**
The lone dive outfitter on the beach, it can take you to Phuket's dive mainstays in the south, but you'll probably choose to visit a few of the nearly two-dozen sites within 15 minutes of the beach. Nearby Ko Waeo is surrounded by vibrant coral, and there's a sunken tin-mining platform, which is also a popular dive. Aqua Divers can also send you on day trips to the Similans.

🧖 WAREE SPA *Spa*
☎ 076 205379; **Th Hat Nai Thon; massages from 400B; ⏲ 9am-9pm**
The spa at this sweet family-owned cottage resort has basic but tasteful environs, a proper Scandinavian sauna and a variety of massages on the menu.

🍴 EAT

🍽 CHAO LAY BISTRO
Thai $$
☎ 076 205500; **www.naithonburi.com**; **9 Moo 4, Tambon Sakhu; ⏲ noon-10.30pm**
Tasty Thai food in a hip, open-air dining room. Try the *panang tha-lay*, prawns or squid in red curry with lime leaves and coconut milk.

🍽 COCONUT TREE
Thai $
34 Th Hat Nai Thon; ⏲ 10am-10pm; 🚻
A homey little place with beach décor, serving grilled lobster and some delicious Thai curries.

🍽 TIEN SENG
Thai $
☎ 084 9481826; **28 Th Hat Nai Thon; ⏲ 8.30am-10.30pm; 🚻 🚻**
Cheap and tasty Thai food and decent American breakfasts are yours at the south end of the beach. Tien Seng fires up the fish grill at night.

🍽 WIWAN
Thai $
☎ 076 205379; fax 076 205381; **22/2 Th Surin; ⏲ 7.30am-10pm, closed during the wet season; 🚻 🚻**
You can try local dishes, like *yum koong siab* (southern-style smoked prawns), or exotic ones, like veggie burgers. Wiwan also has seafood barbecue in the evenings.

HAT NAI YANG & HAT MAI KHAO

Hat Nai Yang has that perfect blend of looks and personality. Its glassy bay is sheltered by a reef that slopes 20m below the surface – which makes for good snorkelling in the dry season and fantastic surfing in the monsoon season. A string of local seafood restaurants and tiki bars line the main beach, which becomes pristine as it stretches north into Sirinat National Park. It's hard to believe you can practically walk to the airport from here.

Phuket's longest beach, Hat Mai Khao, begins within Sirinat National Park, about 5km north of Nai Yang. Sea turtles lay their eggs on the beach here between November and February. A visitors centre with toilets, showers and picnic tables can be found at the main beach area, where you'll also find a huddle of snack shacks and picnic tables in the pines. Take care when swimming. Unlike in sheltered Nai Yang, there's a strong year-round undertow.

 SEE

SIRINAT NATIONAL PARK

☎ 076 328226; www.dnp.go.th; admission 200B

The former Nai Yang National Park and Mai Khao wildlife reserve encompasses 22 sq km of coastal

Picnic among the trees at Sirinat National Park

JOHN GRAY
Tourism pioneer and owner of John Gray's Sea Canoe

What was Ao Phang-Nga like when you launched the Sea Canoe industry in 1987? The habitat was perfect. It was untouched. I would paddle into *hongs* (caves semisubmerged in the sea) that no human had ever explored. **How have things changed?** Within a month of our first copycat starting, the auger molluscs began to disappear. I saw a guide take a bucket of them out of the *hong* and have a barbecue. We've lost white eagles' nests and I once saw three monitor lizards poached for a bottle of whiskey. **What can tourists do to minimise their footprint in Ao Phang-Nga?** Never go on a two-cycle speedboat in the bay. They spew out so much oil you can see it shimmer on the water, which is one of the main reasons the kingfishers have disappeared. They are an indicator species for the health of the entire ecosystem, so this is very disturbing.

BEACHES & TOWNS

UPPER NORTH COAST

land, plus 68 sq km of sea. It runs from the western Phang-Nga provincial border south to the headland that separates Nai Yang from Nai Thon. The beach is absolutely pristine. Sea turtles patrol the reef and lay eggs on the park's northern beaches and on Hat Mai Khao.

YACHT HAVEN PHUKET MARINA

take Yacht Haven turn-off from Hwy 402; admission free

The name doesn't lie. Vessels of all kinds – from 10m speedboats to 50m-plus megayachts – hibernate in this calm harbour surrounded by coastal mountains and channel islands.

DO

DREAM YACHT CHARTER
Watersports

☎ 076 206492; www.dreamyacht charter.com; Yacht Haven Phuket Marina; cruises per person with crew from 41,700B

This international, French-run company charters large bare-boat catamarans with and without crews. They aren't cheap, but sailing between limestone karsts in Ao Phang-Nga is the type of experience worth paying for.

INDIGO SPA *Spa*

☎ 076 327006; www.indigo-pearl.com; Hat Nai Yang; treatments from 1500B; ⏱ 9am-9pm

Set in a 277-room megaresort that doubles as a monument to Phuket's tin-mining past – hardware such as vices, scales and other mining tools are used in the décor down to the tiniest detail – this is a fantastic spa. Treatments include a moist chocolate-pudding scrub, and a pearl wrap featuring vegetal extracts of local cultured pearls.

KITEBOARDING ASIA
Watersports

☎ 081 5914593; www.kiteboarding asia.com; 74/10 Moo 3, Th Hat Nai Yang; lessons from 4000B

CULTURE MINING

Culturally curious developers in and around Phuket have taken cues from the past to create today's hottest resorts, hoping to inspire guests to think a bit deeper about the destination's roots. Six Senses Hideaway Yao Noi (see p129) pays homage to the Andaman Sea's Moken people. Like authentic *chao leh* (sea gypsy) village bungalows, the villas are stilted with thatched roofs and sea views. Of course, the real nomads lacked air-conditioning, butler service and private pools, but that's another matter. Indigo Pearl (see right), on Hat Nai Yang, harks back to the tin-mining days. Huge restored mining works accent the interior along with brushed steel and brass rivets. It's an industrial design that works.

After a chocolate-pudding scrub at Indigo Spa (p123), your worries will dessert you

If you've never tried this up and coming sport, now's your chance. Lessons take place in the sheltered bay and prices include all equipment hire. For a bit more time and money you can become certified by the International Kiteboarding Organisation – a necessary step to be able to hire equipment from most outfitters around the world. Bob, the owner/instructor, also gives traditional surfing lessons (and hires boards) when the swell arrives (best between June and September). The waves here are just as good as in Kata and Nai Han, without the lethal undertow.

🏃 NAUTICA DIVERS
Watersports
☎ 076 328023; www.nauticadivers.com; Hat Nai Yang; dive trips from 2200B
One tank or two? It's your choice if you book trips to the Similans and Phuket's popular dive sites (Shark Point, Anemone, Racha Yai, Racha Noi Phi-Phi) with Nautica.

🏃 OI'S LONGTAIL *Watersports*
☎ 081 9785728; 66 Moo 3, Hat Nai Yang; tours 1600B
Oi specialises in two-hour snorkelling tours of the reefs around Ko Waeo. Cost includes snorkelling gear. He's located at Bank restau-

rant, opposite the long-tail boat harbour.

✈ PARADISE DIVING
Watersports

☎ 076 328278; www.dive-paradise .com; 116 Moo 1, Sakoo Village; dive trips from 2990B

One of the best outfitters on the island, with speedboats on both sides of the north coast, nobody gets you from Phuket to Phi-Phi or the Similans faster than Paradise. As a result, day trips include three tanks and two meals. Paradise offers local dives at Ko Waeo and its shallow house reef, and you can charter its speedboat for tours through gorgeous Ao Phang-Nga.

✈ SALA RESORT & SPA
Spa

☎ 076 338888; www.salaphuket.com; 333 Moo 3, Tambon Maikhao; treatments from 1500B; 🕙 9am-9pm

Enjoy your aromatherapy massage or herbal body scrub at the brand-new (at research time) and absolutely stunning Sala resort. The villa property is a blend of Sino-Portuguese and Art Deco influences with a modern flair. The black-granite infinity pool at the beachfront is gorgeous, and the beachfront bar area includes cushy, circular sofa lounges. It's the kind of place that makes everyone feel like a celebrity.

✈ TAWAN CRUISES
Watersports

☎ 081 943234; www.tawancruises .com; all-inclusive multiday cruises from 236,000B

If five-star luxury sounds better to you than a local long-tail boat, reserve one of Tawan's many motor yachts for custom tours of the Andaman Sea. You choose the destination and it does all the work. Boats depart from Yacht Haven Phuket Marina.

EAT

🍽 BATIK SEAFOOD *Thai* $
88/3 Th Hat Nai Yang;
🕙 10.30am-10pm; ♿ 👶

This beautiful beach-garden restaurant, nestled on the south end of Hat Nai Yang just after the road turns to dust, sports tables beneath thatched gazebos and is surrounded by orchids. It specialises in fresh grilled fish, which it buys from the fish market held just north of the restaurant every afternoon.

🍽 BEACH DINING
Thai $

Hat Nai Yang; 🕙 9am-10pm; ♿ 👶
A strand of Thai seafood shacks (and one pizza joint) huddle together on the middle stretch of Hat Nai Yang. The food is cheap and delicious.

BEACHES & TOWNS

UPPER NORTH COAST

Bust a move at Rebar

♈ DRINK

♈ MR KOBI *Bar*
Hat Nai Yang; ⏲ **11am-1am**
The sign says, 'Broken English spoken here perfect'. But, truthfully, the gregarious Mr Kobi speaks English very well. When the other beach shacks close, Mr Kobi's blender whirs on, and his kitchen doesn't close till the guests go home, or pass out.

★ PLAY

★ REBAR *Club*
☎ **076 327006; www.indigo-pearl.com; Hat Nai Yang; admission free;** ⏲ **5pm-midnight**
Indigo Pearl's hip club, where a DJ spins ambient groove and guests dance on thick and worn timber floors.

★ THE BEACH CLUB *Pub*
88/4 Th Hat Nai Yang; admission free; ⏲ **11am-1am**
This beach pub brings nightlife to sleepy Nai Yang. Happy hour is from 7pm to 8pm and there's live music most nights.

>ISLAND-HOPPING

Long-tail cruising on Ao Phang-Nga

AO PHANG-NGA

Imagine turquoise bays, peppered with over 40 craggy limestone islands, ringed with mangroves and sugar-white beaches, and sprinkled with local fishing villages, and you have conjured the spectacular Ao Phang-Nga. But the secret's out. Tourists in speedboats and kayaks patrol this 400km bay regularly. Part of that is due to the bay's fame. Ko Phing Kan, aka James Bond Island, a sweet limestone droplet that was the plotting assassin's hideout in *The Man with the Golden Gun,* is a popular day trip.

During peak times there can be more traffic than seems reasonable, especially considering that this is supposed to be a national marine park, but if you explore early in the morning or stay out just a bit late, you'll find a slice of sand, sea and limestone karst all of your own.

Fault activity that thrust massive limestone blocks into geometric patterns created the karst scenery. The bay is comprises large and small tidal channels that run through the mangroves and are used by local fishermen as aquatic laneways. Keep an eye out for monitor lizards, white-handed gibbons, crab-eating frogs and sea eagles. Many of the limestone islands feature prehistoric rock art painted or carved onto the walls and ceilings of caves and cliffs. **Khao Khian** (Inscription Mountain) is probably the most visited site. The images depict human figures, fish, crabs, birds and elephants.

The town of Phang-Nga looks and feels a bit rough around the edges, but you won't quibble with its sublime surroundings – it backs up against some sensational limestone cliffs. Everything here to see and do happens in the bay, so you'll need to charter a long-tail boat (easily done with a modicum of haggling) or sign up for an organised tour.

Several food stalls on Phang-Nga's main street sell delicious *khànŏm jiin* (thin wheat noodles) with chicken curry. There's also a small night market on Tuesday, Wednesday and Thursday evenings, just south of Soi Lohakit. Consider Food Safety St – it's 1km beyond the New Lukmuang Hotel, next to the Caltex petrol station. At night it's filled with excellent – and presumably hygiene-conscious – food stalls. **Cha-Leang** (☎ 076 413831; Th Petchkasem; meals 100B) is the best eatery in town. Try the clams with basil leaf and chilli.

Ko Yao Yai and Ko Yao Noi (see p23) are among the most captivating islands in the bay. With a mountainous backbone swathed in rubber plantations, a handful of pristine, turquoise coves dappled with coconut palms, outrageous views of Ao Phang-Nga's jutting limestone islands and a warm, laid-back Muslim population scattered among seven villages, you should plan on spending the night. Yao Noi, the smaller but more populated island, is home to the new Six Senses Hideaway Yao Noi, a swanky five-star resort with pool villas built to resemble an old *chao leh* (sea gypsy) village, and a fab spa. So call ahead for an appointment. Even if you don't spend the night, make sure you eat at **Pradu Seafood** (☎ 076 597015; 46/9 Moo 7, An Pao; ⏰ 11am-10pm). The local chef still fetches ingredients on her motorbike, and makes some of the best fish in southern Thailand.

FAST FACTS
Getting There & Away To get to Phang-Nga town you can hire a car and drive an hour northeast. The route is well marked. Or you can take a bus (80B, 1½ hours, frequent departures) from the bus terminal in Phuket City. There are eight public boats a day shuttling between Phuket's Bang Rong pier and Ko Yao Noi (100B, one to two hours). From there you can take another shuttle boat to Ko Yao Yai (20B, 15 minutes).
Getting Around You can explore Phang-Nga town on foot or by motorcycle taxi. Ko Yao is served by túk-túks (motorised three-wheeled vehicles) for about 80B per ride.
Information Ao Phang-Nga National Park (☎ 076 411136; www.dnp.go.th; ⏰ 8am-4pm)
Tours from Phuket John Gray's Sea Canoe (☎ 076 254505; www.johngray-seacanoe .com; 124 Soi 1, Th Yaowarat, Phuket City; trips 3950-57,800B)
Accommodation Phang-Nga Inn (☎ 076 411963; 2/2 Soi Lohakit; r 400-1600B; ❄); Six Senses Hideaway Yao Noi (☎ 076 418500; www.sixsenses.com/hideaway-yaonoi; r 32,000-74,250B; ❄ 🖳 🍸)

Top left Kayaks navigate the spectacular karst formations of Ao Phang-Nga

KO PHI-PHI

With its arcing blonde beaches, vibrant corals and thick jungles, it's no wonder luscious, limestone Phi-Phi, set in the midst of the Ko Phi-Phi Marine National Park, has once again become the darling of the Andaman coast.

Ko Phi-Phi Don is actually two islands joined by a narrow isthmus that separates the two prized beaches of **Ao Ton Sai** and **Ao Lo Dalam**. **Hat Yao** faces south and has some of Phi-Phi Don's best coral reefs and one of its most impressive swimming beaches. The beautifully languid eastern bays of **Hat Laem Thong** and **Ao Lo Bakao** are reserved for top-shelf resorts, while the smaller bays of **Hat Phak Nam**, **Hat Rantee** and **Ao Toh Ko** are peopled by the bungalow backpacker set.

Diving is the main attraction here, as there are dozens of reefs within reach. Scuba traffic can get thick in the high season, as tourists from Krabi to Phuket all arrive on two-storey boats ready to plunge. But the upside is obvious. There are resident turtles, leopard, bamboo and black-tip reef sharks and, if you're really lucky, whale sharks swimming around spectacular, healthy reef systems.

Ko Phi-Phi Leh, a haven for snorkellers and divers, and setting for the Hollywood film, *The Beach* (p160)

Snorkellers and beginner divers will enjoy the relatively shallow reefs around **Ko Phi-Phi Leh**, an undeveloped island just off the coast of the two-headed Phi-Phi Don. And you can also dive out at **Hin Daeng** and **Hin Muang**, 60km off Ko Phi-Phi, and among Thailand's best sites.

There's also some damn good **climbing** on Ko Phi-Phi, where peak views are spectacular. The main climbing areas are **Ton Sai Tower**, at the western edge of Ao Ton Sai, and **Hin Taak**, a short long-tail boat ride around the bay. There are at least six good climbing shops on the island, and most places charge around 900B for a half-day of climbing or 1600B for a full day, including instruction and gear.

If you're more hiker than climber, take the short, but strenuous, trail to the **Phi-Phi viewpoint**. It's a 305m vertical climb that includes hundreds of steep steps and narrow twisting paths. The views of the marine national park are outrageous – who knew there were this many shades of blue? From here you can head over the hill through the jungle to the peaceful eastern beaches for a DIY snorkelling tour.

With all that activity you will need some fuel. **Chao Koh** (☎ 075 601083; dishes 80-300B; ☺ 10am-10pm) is an open-air seafood restaurant right on the beach with ice rafts stacked with fresh catch. Romantic **Ciao Bella** (Ao Lo Dalam) twinkles with candles and serves authentic Italian and Thai food while lapping waves serenade. If it's a beverage you seek, come to **Carpe Diem** (☎ 048 401219; Hat Hin Khom). The upstairs lounge is a good spot for a sundowner, and you can rock into the night with fire shows, dance parties and live music on the beach.

FAST FACTS

Getting There & Away Ferries leave from Tha Rasada near Phuket City for Phi-Phi at 8.30am, 1.30pm and 2.30pm, and return from Ko Phi-Phi at 9am, 2.30pm and 3pm (400B, 1¾ to two hours).

Getting Around There are no roads on Ko Phi-Phi Don, so you'll be walking. Long-tail boats can be chartered at Ao Ton Sai for short hops around Ko Phi-Phi Don and Ko Phi-Phi Leh.

Information Diving Thailand (www.diving-thailand.org)

Tours from Phuket Offspray Leisure (☎ 081 8941274; www.offsprayleisure.com; 43/87 Chalong Plaza, Rawai; trips 5 days a week from 2950B); Paradise Diving (☎ 076 328278; www.dive-paradise.com; 116 Moo 1, Sakoo Village, Hat Nai Yang; trips 7990B)

Accommodation Ao Toh Ko Beach (☎ 081 5370528; tohkobeach@yahoo.com; bungalows 500-2000B); Zeavola (☎ 075 627024; www.zeavola.com; bungalows 14,000-26,000B; ⛶ 💻 🏊)

KRABI & RAILAY

At first, quirky Krabi feels more like a tourist way station than a destination. From here it's easy to reach several beach and island destinations, including Ko Phi-Phi and the gorgeous beaches of Railay, by public boat. But before you skip town you have some exploring to do.

If you're a climber, it's possible to scale one of the two limestone massifs of **Khao Khanap Nam**, just north of the town centre. Human skeletons, thought to be the remains of people trapped during an ancient flood, were found in the caves here. You'll need to charter a long-tail boat from Khong Kha pier for about 300B to reach the cliff.

The 50-sq-km **Khao Phanom Bencha National Park**, just 20km north of Krabi on Hwy 4, is an even more thrilling sight. On the spine of this 1350m mountain is a virgin swathe of rainforest, a cave with shimmering stalactites and stalagmites, and three major waterfalls. The 11-tier **Huay To Falls** is awesome in the wet season. The park is ribboned with trails, so bring your hiking boots. You can get here from Krabi by túk-túk or motorbike taxi.

Wat Tham Seua (Tiger Cave Temple), 8km northeast of Krabi, is another must-see. The main *wíhǎan* (hall) is built into a long, shallow limestone cave. On either side of the cave, dozens of *kùtì* (monastic cells) are built into various cliffs and caves. You may see a troop of monkeys roaming the grounds.

The most shocking thing about Wat Tham Seua is found in the large main cave. Alongside large portraits of Ajan Jamnien Silasettho, the wat's abbot, are close-up pictures of human entrails and internal organs, which are meant to remind guests of the impermanence of the body. And in a little valley behind the ridge where the *bòt* (central sanctuary) is located, you'll come to a steep stairway leading to a 600m karst peak. The fit and fearless will be rewarded with a Buddha statue, a gilded stupa and tremendous views. A second stairway leads to another network of caves.

After sightseeing head to the night market near the Khong Kha pier. The menus may be in English, but the Thai food is authentic and delicious. For drinks hit the saloonlike environs of the **Old West Bar** (Th Chao Fah; ⏰ 1pm-2am).

As soon as you see the dramatic limestone cliffs, pearl-white beaches and aquamarine bays that wrap around the Railay peninsula, you'll wonder why it took you so long to get here. It's part of the mainland, but sheltered by impenetrable cliffs crawling with rock climbers, so you have to take a boat from Krabi to get here. And you won't be alone. Plenty of midrange resorts line the sand, but development is neatly tucked away in the coconut palms and lush gardens, so it doesn't feel cramped.

Adventurers come for the **climbing**, and Railay has Thailand's best. Climbing shops with equipment hire and instruction are not hard to find. At the tip of the headland, abutting the exclusive Rayavadee resort is **Hat Phra Nang**, the sweetest beach on the peninsula. It's an idyllic patch of white sand beneath overhanging limestone, where monkeys climb the vines. If you get restless, and you're not a climber, hire a kayak and paddle from cliff to cliff.

Railay Bay Resort (Hat Rai Leh West; meals 200B) has some of the peninsula's best food and service, but it will cost you. Eat lunch at the **Rock Restaurant** (Hat Rai Leh East; meals 80-120B). It's situated cliffside at the jungle's edge and has amazing views.

FAST FACTS
Getting There & Away Air-conditioned buses and minivans make the three-hour run from Phuket City to Krabi hourly (115B to 250B). Long-tail boats (pictured above) ply the waters from Krabi to Railay from 8am to 6pm (200B, 45 minutes).
Getting Around You can do central Krabi on foot and hire motorbike taxis and túk-túks, or hire your own motorbike if you plan on visiting the outskirts. Railay is roadless. If you need to get from one end of the peninsula to the other, hire a long tail.
Information Railay Thailand (www.railay.com)
Tours from Phuket Limestone Adventures (☎ 076 273328; www.limestoneadventures .com; Phuket Boat Lagoon, 20/16 Moo 2, Th Thepkrasattri; trips from 6100B)
Accommodation Railay Bay Resort (☎ 075 622570; www.railaybayresort.com; bungalows 2900-11,500B; ✷); Rapala Rockwood Resort (☎ 075 622586; rapala@loxinfo.co.th; bungalows 500-750B)

HAT KHAO LAK

Just before you arrive you'll round a bend and suddenly Khao Lak's vast horseshoe bay, backed by rolling granite hills thick with tropical rainforest, will reveal itself. You'll notice resort rooftops peeking out from the swaying coconut palms and tourists lounging and strolling on the golden sand as the turquoise sea, which hides Thailand's choicest reefs, gently licks the shore in overlapping ovals.

Keep driving through the main drag, however, and you'll soon confront Khao Lak's shadow, in the form of an armoured police boat stranded in an empty field, surrounded by tourists snapping photos. Consider it proof that while there has been significant tourism resurgence since the tsunami, Khao Lak's wounds run deep. Nowhere outside of Aceh, Indonesia, was hit harder on 26 December 2004. But it's that combination of beauty and experience that makes Khao Lak such an amazing place to visit.

The 125-sq-km **Khao Lak-Lam Ru National Park** (☎ 076 420243; www.dnp .go.th; adult/child 200/100B; ☼ 8am-4.30pm), just south of town, is a splendid collection of sea cliffs, mountains, beaches, estuaries, forested valleys and mangroves. The park is home to hornbills, drongos, tapirs, gibbons, monkeys and the seldom-seen Asiatic black bears. Guided treks along the coast or inland can be arranged through many tour agencies in town, as can long-tail boat trips up the scenic **Khlong Thap Liang** estuary. The latter afford opportunities to view mangrove communities of crab-eating macaques. Just north of Khao Lak is a network of sandy beach trails – some of which lead to deserted beaches – which are fun to explore on foot or by hired motorbike. Most of the hotels in town hire motorbikes for 250B per day.

Of course, **diving** is the big draw here, and you'll see dozens of dive shops offering day trips and live aboards to the Similan Islands and Richelieu Rock, among other local sites. You can also book a week-long trip to the Burma banks, where you're likely to have the reefs all to yourself. One of the smaller-scale and more ecologically minded outfitters in the region is **Wicked Diving** (www.wickeddiving.com). It's easily spotted on the main road.

About that road… Khao Lak town, dominated by package tourists and Scandinavian families, isn't especially charming, but if you head for the nearby fishing villages you'll get a whiff of real life on the northern Andaman coast. The closest village, **Baan Nam Kem**, has a moving Tsunami Memorial Park – a black-granite, wave-shaped monument just steps from a stunning white-sand beach. Few tourists ever make it down here. If you'd rather venture into the villages with a guide, **Andaman Discoveries** (☎ 087 9177165; Khuraburi; www.andamandiscoveries.com) runs fabulous community-based tours, which can include homestays, community-service projects and volunteer placement. You create the itinerary and your money is funnelled directly into the community.

If fresh parrot fish rubbed with lemongrass and grilled with pineapple sounds like your kind of meal, head to **Mama's Café** (meals from 120B), next to 7-Eleven in Hat Bang Niang (the town 2.5km north of Khao Lak). Part street-side café, part tiki bar, there's rarely an empty seat in the house. **Coconut Grove** (Th Hat Bang Niang, meals 150-200B) is a great beach-front seafood restaurant and a favourite among the local dive masters. After dinner fall into the funky driftwood environs of **Happy Snapper** (Hwy 4). Owned and run by a once-famous Bangkok bass player, he and his very tight band lay down rock classics six nights a week during the high season.

FAST FACTS

Getting There & Away Hire a car and follow the signs. It's an easy hour's drive north from Phuket. Alternatively, air-conditioned buses from Phuket to Takua Pa (80B, two hours) will stop in Khao Lak if you ask the driver.

Getting Around Walk, hire a motorbike (250B per day) or take túk-túks (about 100B).

Information Khaolak.com (www.khaolak.com)

Accommodation Khaolak Banana Bungalows (☎ 076 485889; www.khaolakbanana.com; 4/147 Moo 7, Kukkak; bungalows 500-1200B; ✕ ☲); The Sarojin (☎ 076 427900; www.sarojin.com; r 12,500-23,250B; ✕ ☲ ☲)

SIMILAN ISLANDS MARINE NATIONAL PARK

Renowned by divers the world over, beautiful Similan Islands Marine National Park is 70km offshore. Its smooth granite islands are as impressive above water as below, topped with rainforest, edged with white-sand beaches and fringed with coral reef.

Two of the nine islands, Island 4 (Ko Miang) and Island 8 (Ko Similan), have ranger stations and accommodation. Park headquarters and most visitor activity centres on Island 4. 'Similan' comes from the Malay word *sembilan,* meaning nine, and while each island is named, they're commonly referred to with numbers.

Pardon the cliché, but the Similans are a **diving** paradise. There are seamounts (at **Fantasy Rocks**), rock reefs (at **Ko Payu**) and dive-throughs (at **Hin Pousar**; 'Elephant-head'), with marine life ranging from tiny plume worms and soft corals to schooling fish and whale sharks. There are dive sites at each of the six islands north of Ko Miang; the southern part of the park (Islands 1, 2 and 3) is off limits to divers and is a turtle-nesting ground. No facilities for divers exist in the national park itself, so you'll need to book a trip with an outfitter in Hat Khao Lak or Phuket. The best islands for diving are Island 9, which has excellent coral slopes, and Islands 5 and 6.

Snorkelling is good at several points around Island 4, especially in the main channel, and on Islands 7 and 8. You can hire snorkel gear from the park (per day 100B), and most dive operators offer inexpensive snorkelling options.

The forest around park headquarters on Ko Miang has a couple of **walking** trails and some great wildlife. The fabulous Nicobar pigeon, with its wild mane of grey-green feathers, is common here. Endemic to the islands of the Andaman Sea, it's one of 39 bird species in the park. Hairy-legged land crabs and flying foxes (or fruit bats) are relatively easily seen in the forest, as are flying squirrels. In fact, if you camp, you may be dozing beneath them.

A small **beach track**, with information panels, leads 400m to a tiny, pretty snorkelling bay. Detouring from it, the **Viewpoint Trail** – 500m or so of steep scrambling – has panoramic vistas from the top. A 500m walk to **Sunset Point** takes you through forest to a smooth granite platform facing west.

On Ko Similan (pictured below) there's a 2.5km forest hike to a **viewpoint**, and a shorter, steep scramble off the main beach to the top of **Sail Rock**.

FAST FACTS

Getting There & Away There's no public transport to the park, but independent travellers can book a speedboat transfer (return 1700B, 1½ hours) with a day-trip operator from Khao Lak and book passage back to the mainland with the national park office.

Getting Around No cars and no roads mean you're walking, swimming or boating in the Similans.

Information National Park, Wildlife & Plant Conservation Department (www.dnp.go.th)

Tours from Phuket Paradise Diving (☎ 076 328278; www.dive-paradise.com; 116 Moo 1, Sakoo Village, Hat Nai Yang; trips 7990B); The Junk (☎ 076 284568; www.thejunk.com; 6 Th Koktanod, Hat Kata; multiday trips from US$1250)

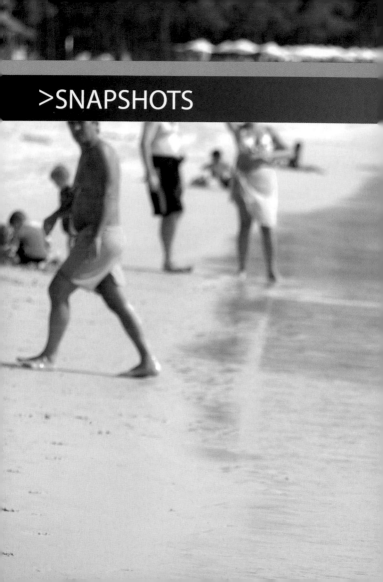

>SNAPSHOTS

Phuket favours the adventurous. From coral reefs and monsoon swells to animal encounters, succulent night markets and hilltop temples, there is a tonne to see and do. Don't be a spectator. Get wet. Make an offering. Rummage through the antique shops, and eat as much as possible.

It's not widely known, but elephants also vacation on Phuket's beaches

ACCOMMODATION

There are a dozen ways to sleep in Phuket, from stylish self-catering apartments to zenned-out holiday homes to countless five-star resorts. Some of those are the big names. Amanpuri, part of the Aman Resort family, continues to attract the ultrarich. Le Meridian and the emerging Six Senses Hideaway brand (with its high ecological standards and top-shelf spas) both have multiple luxury properties in the Phuket orbit.

Several Thai-owned properties are also worth looking into. Mom Tri, the architect and owner of the Boathouse (p81) and Villa Royale (see boxed text, p78), was one of the first to develop the Hat Kata (p74) coast. Thank him when you admire the trees that ring the beach. He saved them from the saw (see boxed text, p78). And the new Sala resort in Hat Mai Khao (p121) is a stunning rendition of Sino-Portuguese Art Deco.

All this money and luxury development comes at a time when Phuket is enjoying a golden age in tourism. Even with more rooms than ever before, during the high season it can be impossible to find one. Which is why budget travellers are feeling squeezed. Below-standard guesthouses can cost over 1500B per night, but there's a way around the price crunch.

First, you have to select the location that suits you best. Hat Patong (p52) is the most densely populated resort area. It's got the hottest nightlife, some terrific dining and the beaches are packed all day. But it can feel like uni days revisited. Hat Kata and Hat Karon (p70) cater to Scandinavian package tourists, but it's generally a fun, young crowd. Kata's beaches are gorgeous and there are some terrific boutique hotels in the area.

Need a place to stay? Find and book it at lonelyplanet.com. Fifty properties are featured for Phuket — each personally visited, thoroughly reviewed and happily recommended by a Lonely Planet author. From hostels to high-end hotels, we've hunted out the places that will bring you unique and special experiences. Read independent reviews by authors and other travellers, and get practical information including amenities, maps and photos. Then reserve your room simply and securely via Hotels & Hostels — our online booking service. It's all at lonelyplanet.com/hotels.

Reasonable Hat Kamala (p98), just north of Patong, is perfect for long-term and self-catering guests. Hat Surin (p101) is a chic spot, sprinkled with five-star properties and beachfront dining. You'd do well to base here if you have the cash. It's slow at night, but Patong is only a short taxi ride away.

Ao Bang Thao (p106) is in awkward transition from fishing village to resort and villa mecca – it's not uncommon to see buffalo grazing between construction sites. Its beaches are superb.

Further up the coast the beaches get even better and more secluded. If you're looking for a quiet, shoes-optional retreat, try Hat Nai Thon (p120), Hat Nai Yang (p121) or Hat Mai Khao (p121).

Hiring a house in Rawai (p84) is the best option for long-termers and self-caterers. The beaches are lovely, the eating is great, and the community is engaging and fun. And it's only a short drive from Phuket City (p38).

Location decided, sort through your online options. Book a room or rental well in advance. If you're an unrepentant backpacker, who we love by the way, you'll be relegated to the budget haunts of Phuket's Old Town (see p38). Of course, that also happens to be the centre of Baba culture, surrounded by fantastic architecture, shopping and food, so you'll be fine.

WEB RESOURCES

Useful websites for hotels on Phuket include www.phuket-hotels.com, www.phukethotels.com and www.phuket.com. If you're interested in rental options, check out www.phuketpremierproperty.com, www.siam realestate.com and www.indigore.com.

BEST BEACH MOD HABITAT
> Sala Resort & Spa (www.salaphuket .com)
> Mövenpick (www.movenpick-hotels .com)
> BYD Lofts (www.bydlofts.com)

BEST THAI TRADITIONALISTS
> Villa Royale (www.villaroyalephuket .com)
> Amanpuri (www.amanresorts.com)
> Twin Palms (www.twinpalms-phuket .com)

BEST ANTHROPOLOGICAL MEMORY
> Indigo Pearl (www.indigo-pearl.com)
> Six Senses Hideaway Yao Noi (www .sixsenses.com)
> Thalang Guesthouse (talanggh@ phuket.ksc.co.th)

BEST VALUE
> Newspaper (www.newspaper-phuket .com)
> Baipho & Baitong (www.baipho.com)
> Rawai Beach Resort (www.rawai beachresort.com)

DIVING

One of the principal attractions of Phuket lies beneath the surface of the Andaman Sea. That's where you'll find coral walls, slopes and bommies teeming with so many varieties of fish, from fingernail-sized pygmy sea-horses to regal whale sharks, you'll think you were caught in some kind of Technicolor blizzard.

Most dive centres focus on nine major dive sites scattered south and east of Ao Chalong, with maximum depths from 24m to 40m. Shark Point, named for the leopard sharks that cruise the sandy bottom, is likely to catch your attention when you first scan the map. That's understandable. Sharks have a certain star quality. But the site also features three pinnacles dense with marine life, including a stunning array of sea fans and sponges.

Leopard sharks also tend to hug the coral wall off the coast of Ko Dok Mai, where you can explore two caves. Anemone Reef is a good beginners dive. The top of the reef is smothered in sea anemone, and you'll see a number of juvenile moray eels as well. King Cruiser is an old car ferry that bottomed on Anemone Reef and split in two in 1997. Daylight penetrates a majority of the wreck. Coral Island is mostly a training site for new divers, but it has some of the healthiest corals in the area, which attract a rich diversity of sea life. And there are two sites each off the coast of Ko Racha Noi and Ko Racha Yai.

The reef off the southern tip of Racha Noi is particularly good for experienced divers. It's a deep site where soft corals cling to boulders, around which pelagic fish species, like barracuda, rainbow runners and trevally, roam. Manta and marble rays are also frequently glimpsed here, and if you're lucky, you may even see a whale shark.

Reef sharks tend to visit the northern tip of Ko Racha Noi, a great multi-level dive site, which also makes it an easy mark for lazy outfitters who do the one-stop drop regardless of group experience. Leopard sharks and hawksbill turtles are occasionally seen on the eastern side of Ko Racha Yai, which is superior to the site at Bungalow Bay on the other side of the island.

If you're staying on the northern half of the island, you should also consider half-day trips to Ko Waeo, an emerging dive site for outfitters based in Hat Surin (p101) all the way up to Hat Nai Yang (p121). Turtles and huge puffer fish congregate at this vibrant coral reef. There's also an interesting tin-mining wreck (a sunken mining platform) nearby.

Phuket is perfectly situated between two marine national parks, which are two of Thailand's dive meccas. Ko Phi-Phi (p130) has nearly a dozen dive sites surrounding this tiny limestone archipelago. Dive traffic can get thick here in the high season, but you'll deal with that in order to hang with resident turtles and leopard, bamboo and black-tip reef sharks.

Of course, the region's best diving is found 30 nautical miles from the mainland in the reefs around the Similan Islands, protected as the Similan Islands Marine National Park (p136). The diving here is so good that most divers ditch day trips in favour of multiday live aboards where divers can rack up close to 20 dives in five days.

The Similans are two-faced. The east side is sheltered, with white sand, idyllic turquoise coves, and reefs dense with soft corals and teeming with fish. The rugged west is another matter. There is no land between here and Africa, so currents tend to be strong, which at times clears gaps in the boulders for some unbelievable tunnel swims. The best time to dive the Similans is during late March and early April, when plankton blooms attract the pelagics, including reef and whale sharks and eagle and manta rays. For more info log onto www.phuket-guide.net/phuket_diving/index.htm.

Clown anemonefish treat divers to a vivid splash of colour

FOOD

Dining in Phuket is an embarrassment of riches. Across the spectrum of price and cuisine you will find something to satisfy you. There is an innumerable amount of fresh seafood grills on this island, and nearly every one of them allows you to survey and select your catch.

Of course, Phuket has more residents who were born elsewhere in Thailand than natives, and these folks brought their own take on Thai cuisine with them. *Larb,* a minced chicken, beef or pork salad mixed with chilli, mint and coriander is always delicious.

When the subject of Thai food pops up, most people conjure an image of the world's greatest noodle dish, *pàt tai*. It's made from rice noodles stir-fried with fish sauce, chilli and egg in a red-hot wok. Some add prawns, chicken or tofu, along with a dash of vinegar, radish and a crumbled peanut garnish. One of south Thailand's regional specialities is *massaman* curry, which is best made with beef or duck, seared on a grill, then slow cooked in a stew of potatoes, coconut milk, fish and tamarind sauce, and accented by cinnamon and cardamom.

The local Baba people have relied on homemade noodles with fresh seafood as a staple. They augment it with curries and interesting prawn dishes. You can have them raw in a broth of lime and chilli or smoked and stewed in a spicy curry. The Baba also do wonderful things with sugar and nuts, so be sure to visit Cookie House (p46) in Phuket's Old Town.

Strangely, Italian food has taken off in Phuket. La Gaetana (in Phuket's Old Town; p46) and Da Vinci (in Rawai; p92) are two of the best. Fusion is also rampant, and some of the best restaurants on the island blend Thai and European influences seamlessly.

And then there's the street food. You can find it in night markets, in dark sweaty *soi* (lanes or small streets) off Th Bangla and in a rambling shack by the roadside. The rule of thumb is to turn off that fearful inner dialogue, trust what you see and what you smell, and order liberally.

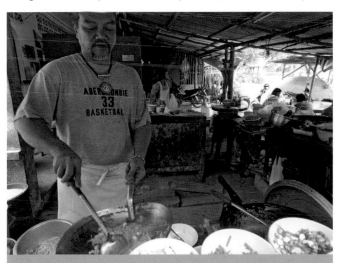

BEST STREET FOOD IN PHUKET
> Som Tum Lanna (p94)
> Fried Chicken (p62)
> Rawai Seafood Grills (p93)
> The Pad Thai Shop (p73)
> Patong Food Park (p63)

BEST FOR FUSION
> Siam Indigo (p46)
> The Boathouse (p81)
> China Inn (p45)
> Mom Tri's Kitchen (p80)
> Tatonka (p110)

Top left Deep-fried shrimp fritters for sale at a morning market **Above** Chef making *pàt tai* at Hat Karon

SURFING

Phuket is an undercover surf paradise. Once the monsoons bring their mid-year swell, glassy seas fold into barrels. The best waves arrive between June and September, when Hat Kata (p74) becomes the surfing capital of Phuket. An annual competition is held here in late August or early September, and this is also where **Phuket Surf** (www.phuketsurf.com) is based. The best waves on Kata are found at the south end, and they typically top out at 2m. Hat Nai Han (see p84) can get huge (up to 3m) near the yacht club. Be warned, both Kata and Nai Han have vicious undertows that can claim lives.

Hat Kalim, just north of Patong, is sheltered and has a consistent break that also gets up to 3m. **The Phuket Boardriders Club** (www.phuketboardriders .com) sponsors an August contest here. Hat Kamala's (p98) northernmost beach has a nice 3m break, and Laem Singh, just up the coast in front of the Amanpuri resort, gets very big and fast, plus it's sheltered from wind by the massive headland.

Hat Nai Yang (p121) may have the best waves in all of Phuket. They are more than 200m offshore, so you'll have to paddle a bit, but the reef provides a consistent break, swells get up to 3m and there is no undertow. Because surfing isn't a major draw to the island, there are few places to get lessons and hire boards. But if you bring your own stick and skills, and arrive with the wind, you'll find some nice waves all the way up the west coast.

Once the monsoon arrives, so do the waves

BARS & CLUBS

About the only things more available on the island than fresh seafood are cocktails. In fact, there are almost too many bars and pubs, which tends to thin out the crowds. And yes, part of the problem is that there is no shortage of karaoke bars with twinkling lights and come-hither hostesses. But sundowners will always beckon, and good nights out, without all that bar-girl baggage, can be found.

The best place to swill to the setting sun is at After Beach Bar (p82), above Kata. The view is sublime, pina coladas are made with fresh coconut water and served in coconut shells, the crowds are consistent and Bob Marley makes everything feel good.

When the night deepens, you should step to Phuket's Old Town (see p38). Timber Hut (pictured below; p49) is a fantastic night out with great live music and a local (mostly Thai) scene. Arrive early if you want a seat; otherwise be ready to dance in cramped corners. Ka Jok See (p48) is a restaurant that morphs into a bohemian after-party every night. It has exceptional music and resident hostesses who make damn sure you dance. Patong is the obvious party choice. But don't get mired on lust lane (aka Th Bangla). Two Black Sheep (p66) has terrific live rock music and a good crowd most nights. And when it's time to groove, head to Club Lime (p67). That's where the pretty party people let loose.

Music, whiskey and wood, the Timber Hut (p49) has all the elements of a great night out

SPAS, RETREATS & MASSAGE

There should be a two-massage minimum for all tourist arrivals in Phuket. Few destinations have the combination of massage quality, price and availability that Phuket has. The island is sprinkled with local shopfront massage joints that are extremely therapeutic. They offer traditional Thai massage (a yogic-like therapy in which you're folded and stretched a thousand ways), oil massage (think deep tissue), aromatherapy massage (an oil massage with an herbal extract kick to induce deep relaxation) and reflexology (where a foot massage meets shiatsu).

One of the best of the shopfront spas can be found at Herbal Steam Sauna (p88) in Rawai. Not only does it offer massages, but you will prepare your body and lungs beforehand by steeping in a traditional, wood-fired herbal sauna.

If grassroots massage feels too gritty for you, upgrade to The Sense Spa (p78) in Kata or Let's Relax (p56) in Patong. Both offer polished environs and an array of scrubs and wraps. And if you're looking for a luxurious spa experience, check out the Six Senses Hideaway Yao Noi (pictured below; see p129). Its brand-new Erawan Destination Spa in Ao Phang-Nga, just minutes from Phuket, is perfect for those hungry for a wellness infusion of nutrition, yoga, t'ai chi and meditation. Plus, the company has a passionate ecological ethos (see boxed text, p123). Those looking to kick-start a healthy lifestyle change can also combine yoga, massage and fasting at Atsumi Healing (p88) in Rawai.

Pamper yourself at Six Senses Hideaway Yao Noi

PHUKET FOR KIDS

If you travel to Phuket with children, you'll quickly find out that the hospitable Thais go even further out of their way for guests with little ones in tow. Restaurant managers don't cower at the sight of young families, and hotel staff will shower them with treats. Plus, there's a fabulous range of activities for kids of all ages.

Water sports hold an obvious appeal, and kids 13 and over can learn to dive. Toddlers will feel comfortable in the shallow tidal lagoon at Hat Nai Han (see p84), a favourite playground of local families at sunset. Young animal lovers will enjoy Phuket Zoo (p44), which has monkeys, elephants and crocodiles, as well as a butterfly farm. A royal ride atop a friendly elephant at the Kok Chang Safari (p76) is bound to please. They may also enjoy meeting the friendly Charlie, a handsome monkey who you'll find at the bar. Or he may just find you. The Phuket Aquarium (p51) and the Phuket Gibbon Rehabilitation Centre (p114) are also interesting for older children, and a trip to the monkey platform on Ko Sireh (see p50), where you'll see nearly 100 monkeys emerge from the mangroves at sunset, is always exciting.

Families also get force fed tickets to Phuket Fantasea (p98), a pricey extravaganza of wild animals, costumed dance, special effects, pyrotechnics, lousy dinner and magic (marvel at the disappearing elephants) – but it's very cheesy. You'll get more giggles from a simple túk-túk (motorised three-wheeled vehicle) ride along the coast. Check out www.1stopphuket.com/about_phuket/children/for tips.

Pint-sized archaeologists excavate on Hat Bang Thao

GAY & LESBIAN PHUKET

The epicentre of Phuket's open and socially integrated gay community can be found along the network of streets that link the Royal Paradise Hotel with Th Rat Uthit in Hat Patong (p52). This is where you'll find most of the hotels and bars that cater to gay clientele, but just because there is widespread acceptance doesn't mean you'll see a lot of public displays of affection here. That's considered a cultural no-no for couples of any ilk.

The Boat Bar was the first prominent nightspot for gay men in Patong, and it remains the island's only gay disco. It receives a blend of men and women, both gay and straight. There's a nightly cabaret show at midnight. My Way is a more laid-back bar with cabaret shows, and the modern Spartacus is centrally located and always attracts a crowd.

But it's not all about the bars. The Phuket Gay Festival is considered by many to be the best in Thailand, maybe even Southeast Asia. It's typically held over a weekend between February and April; the dates fluctuate from year to year, so check ahead to make sure. The main events of this four-day weekend party are a huge beach volleyball tournament and the Grand Parade, featuring floats, cheering crowds and beautiful costumes in the streets of Patong. In recent years the festival has also included social responsibility campaigns, such as HIV awareness, staying clean and sober, and the fight against child prostitution. Check www.gaypatong .com for more information.

Check out the costumes and floats at the Grand Parade

TEMPLES & SHRINES

What is a wat? Well, it's a temple, and you haven't really experienced Thailand until you've walked on hallowed grounds. Unlike Bangkok and Chiang Mai, Phuket's Buddhist temples lack the centuries of history, but the symbolism is there – think gold-leaf saturated Buddha figures and green- and gold-mosaic serpents – and they are often suffused with incense plumes and buzz with ritual.

Wat Chalong (pictured below; p88), situated just off the main highway, is the most visited temple, but Wat Phra Thong (p115) is more interesting, with dozens of shrines promising health, wealth, success and love to those who ritualise. The reclining Buddha (see p50) at Ko Sireh is massive and so are the fantastic views from the hilltop. And still other compounds host residential monks who meditate and chant at sunrise and sunset.

Phuket's Old Town has several Chinese shrines. Bang Niew Shrine (p40) is a relatively new complex (built 1934) that hosts occasional Chinese opera productions, and a certain Taoist mystery has penetrated deep into the bones of the arresting Shrine of Serene Light (p43). And being southern Thailand, there are some lovely mosques whose warbled call lures in hundreds of seekers dressed in flowing white robes. Check out this long-time local's blog for temple tips: www.jamie-monk.blogspot.com.

BEST TRADITIONAL TEMPLES & SHRINES
> Shrine of Serene Light (p43)
> Wat Phra Thong (p115)
> Wat Sireh (p50)
> Wat Thep Watnaram (p116)
> Masjid Mukaram Bang Tao (p101)

BEST ALTERNATIVE PRAYER SITES
> Big Buddha (p74)
> Elephant Shrine (p86)
> Good Luck Shrine (p54)

SHOPPING & MARKETS

There are so many rickety, makeshift shopping stalls run by shameless hawkers in Phuket's resort areas that it can discourage even the most dedicated consumer. Although at first glance you may see a lot for sale but not a lot to buy, don't be fooled, there are treasures here.

Cultured pearls, sapphires and rubies are all mined in Thailand, so you can find some exceptional deals on precious stones. The pearls are the best bargain. There are also some sensational antiques. Heritage Collection (p103) has the best gallery. Baanboonpitak (p60) in Patong is less fabulous, but it's dusty and gritty and lots of fun to rummage through.

Outside the two major malls, Central Festival and Jung Ceylon (p61), Phuket City (p44) is best for designer clothes. Most come from independent designers and you can have dresses and suits custom made here as well. Go to Patong (see p60) for a handmade pashmina or a Kashmiri rug.

And if you're into food, don't miss Phuket's many local markets. The morning market at Mae Ubol (p54) and Banzaan Shopping Plaza (p60) are both a hive of local energy, and Phuket has dozens of night markets. Bring an appetite when you see the stalls sprout on the street corners. This is where noodles, chicken, curries and fish sizzle, smoke and stew, and locals come to eat, drink and shop under the streetlights.

BEST FASHION & TEXTILE BOUTIQUES
> Island Paradise (p44)
> The Royal King Collection (p61)
> Ban Boran Textiles (p44)
> Lilac (p45)
> Cháco (p44)

BEST FOOD MARKETS
> Chalong Night Market (p92)
> Rawai Night Market (p93)
> Mae Ubol Market (p54)
> Downtown Plaza Market (p44)
> Banzaan Shopping Plaza (p60)

>BACKGROUND

Monk at Wat Karon (p70)

BACKGROUND

HISTORY

Phuket's backstory reads like an old-school Robert Louis Stevenson adventure novel. It features, among other things, jungle-dwelling pygmies, savvy Indian and European merchants, (supposedly) marauding sea gypsies, immigrant Chinese tin miners, and cross-dressing war heroines that helped save Thailand from Burma's imperial lust. Yeah, it's safe to say Phuket has a past.

The island has always welcomed foreigners. Phuket City was actually founded in the 1st century BC by Indian merchants. Ptolemy, a Greek geographer who visited in the 3rd century AD, dubbed it 'Jang Si Lang', which later became 'Junk Ceylon', the name you'll find on ancient maps of Thailand.

Among Phuket's original locals were now-extinct primitive tribes similar to Malaysia's surviving Semang pygmies. They lived in triple-canopy virgin rainforest and survived by hunting and eating jungle fruits and roots. Meanwhile, nomads of Malay descent, known today as *chao leh* (sea gypsies), populated the coastal areas of Phuket. They sailed from cove to cove and island to island in hardy houseboats that could weather the roughest seas, living off shellfish and turtle soup, fishing for pearls and staying until the beach's resources were depleted. They then moved on.

They also had a reputation for piracy, which struck fear into captains of merchant ships. An early French Jesuit missionary believed it impossible to go 'more than half a league from [Phuket] without life and property being endangered by bandits'. Of course, it is impossible to verify the *chao leh*'s 'crimes', and it's just as likely that it was their animist belief system that sent fear rushing through the bones of the Christian and Muslim merchants. Real or imagined, this reputation may explain why, even though a number of ships sheltered in Phuket's bays during monsoon season for centuries, it took so long for permanent trading and mining settlements to be established on the island.

But eventually the lure of tin won out and Portuguese, then French, then British traders descended in the 16th century. A century later the British contemplated using Phuket as a base from which they could control the strategically vital Malacca Straits. They sent Captain Francis Light to scout it out, and he was swept up in Phuket's most important historical event.

The year was 1785 and Burma and Thailand were locked in a series of wars for regional supremacy. Thai soldiers had repelled Burmese forces from Phuket a year earlier, but now the Burmese were returning in an enormous fleet. Captain Light spotted them and alerted the governor's office. But the governor had recently passed away, so his wife, Kunying Jan, took charge. She and her sister, Mook, assembled the forces and, according to legend, disguised local women as male soldiers, which made Phuket's military manpower seem invincible to the Burmese scouts. They attacked anyway, but quickly lost heart and left after a short siege. King Rama I awarded Kunying Jan with the royal title of 'Thao Thep Kasattri', and she and her sister are honoured with the Heroines Monument at the Thalang roundabout.

In the early 19th century the tin-mining boom took Phuket by storm and attracted thousands of Chinese labourers. The Chinese brought their culinary and spiritual traditions with them, and when they intermarried with the Thai, a new culture was born. The first and future generations of the ethnic Thai-Chinese are known as the Baba people. Although their roots were in the mines, many Baba descendents became merchants. They built up Phuket City, erecting enormous homes with Portuguese and Chinese accents, high ceilings and thick walls so they would remain cool. These impressive structures and their Baba inhabitants are the main attractions of Phuket's Old Town.

However, the birth of one culture meant another disappeared. With the advent and replication of tin-mining camps, the pygmy tribes became marginalised. Anthropologists believe the last of the pygmies were displaced in the mid-19th century.

Tin, along with rubber, remained the dominant industry in Phuket until the 1970s, when the beachcombers began arriving en masse after Club Med invested in Hat Kata and Thai Airways began offering daily flights from Bangkok. Mom Tri, an architect distantly related to the royal family, designed the Club Med resort (see boxed text, p78).

Tourism remained strong until the tsunami hit on 26 December 2004. On Phuket 250 people died as Patong, Kamala, Kata, Karon, Nai Thon and Nai Yang all suffered major damage. But Khao Lak and Ko Phi-Phi were hit much harder. Official estimates have Thailand's death toll at 5300, but those involved with rescue and recovery efforts believe the actual number is far greater. As a result of the disaster, Phuket's economy suffered in the short term, but in 2006 resort development skyrocketed and shows no signs of slowing down.

THE PHUKET LIFESTYLE

Phuket is an island of dreams. And not just for tourists. Expatriate and Thai investors, immigrant labourers from the ethnic provinces of Myanmar (Burma), Bangkok artists and the imported Thai service staff who come from the country's forgotten northeast all arrive here to make their mark. Some imagine a fortune or fantasise about their tropical retirement; others are simply looking for the promise of a steady pay cheque to share with their struggling families or are escaping a hellish reality in their native land.

Most of the expats are resort managers, restaurateurs, dive masters or retirees. And while there is some overlap among them, expat cliques are often defined by where they live, which makes sense considering the island's size.

Tourists drop a lot of coin in Phuket, but the service sector earns frighteningly low wages. In most cases these staff work six days a week, but some employers (usually callous expat business owners) demand that they work seven days a week during the high season, which lasts more than three months. A lot of the bar girls were sent here by their parents and initially worked in low-wage service jobs, but quickly realised much more money could be made providing a different sort of service to the midlife-crises set.

Phuket locals also get into the tourism action. The long-tail boat captains, túk-túk (motorised three-wheeled vehicle) drivers, the gregarious guys who run the jet-ski concessions and many of the local restaurant owners were born and raised here. Some are Buddhist, many are Muslim, and almost all are observant. But unlike the hot spots in the south, religious conflict is nonexistent.

Phuket City is where middle-class locals (and their number is growing) prefer to shop, sip and dine. Many of them come from Phuket families who have lived here for generations, and work in white-collar office jobs or own small businesses. Phuket's Old Town is also an emerging arts district. Artists and designers from Bangkok and Phuket have rented live-work studio and gallery space in Sino-Portuguese relics, adding an interesting creative flavour to these historic streets.

Back in the resort districts, you'll also meet shop owners and tailors from India or Nepal, and others who appear to be of Indian descent and are Hindu, but actually come from Myanmar's Kachin State, which is routinely terrorised by Myanmar's military junta. Most of the Kachin were brought here when they were 12 as indentured servants to Thai families. They were promised school, but instead were put to work selling knock-offs and pirated DVDs to tourists. They have a great spirit, speak English, Thai, Burmese and Kachin, and are more than willing to share their stories.

And there is another, silent segment of the Phuket social scene. They are the carpenters, masons and fishermen. The builders are often migrant workers from Myanmar, and they are here to put up hotels and holiday homes just as fast as they can. The fishermen grew up here, and so did their parents and grandparents. When we sleep, they are working. When we're getting ready to eat their catch for dinner, most of them are already dreaming.

ART & ARCHITECTURE

The charming Sino-Portuguese relics in Phuket's Old Town take you back 110 years to when European tin-mining corporations built the town's roads and canals, and the Hokkien Chinese merchant class and labour force erected the sturdy old buildings to reflect European sophistication and Chinese style. Two designs stand out: the Sino-Portuguese shop-house and the Sino-Colonial mansion.

The front of the shophouse was a commercial zone, while the court-yard space housed a water well and doubled as the family gathering area. The bedrooms were upstairs. Those with an eye for detail will notice Corinthian, Ionic and Doric embellishments, while the doors and windows have Chinese accents, like carved teak louvres and inlaid doors.

Several Chinese merchants did quite well during the tin boom and they built Sino-Colonial mansions, aka *angmor lao,* featuring a capacious portico, a terrace on the upper floor and multiple courtyards, each equipped with a well, from which servants would fetch water for the interior bathrooms. There are still a few mansions standing, haunted yet regal, along Th Krabi.

During our research trip, the Old Phuket Foundation was restoring and revitalising the old façades. They were hiding the spider web of electrical wires that obscured the 2nd-floor windows, and offering owners and residents a free paint job. The idea is to transform the old town into an architectural destination and hopefully jumpstart the small business economy (see boxed text, p42).

It certainly helps that many excellent young artists and designers, from Bangkok and Phuket, have turned some of the shophouses on

Th Thalang into live-work studio galleries, while others have become fashionable cafés and restaurants. Most of Phuket's Old Town art has obvious natural and traditional Buddhist influences, but there's usually a distinctively modern twist. Rawai is also home to a half-dozen artist-owned galleries. They lack the romantic location of the Old Town, but there's good work here, too. The mixed media at Red Gallery (p86) is particularly intriguing.

GOVERNMENT & POLITICS

Thailand's national government is based on the UK's constitutional monarchy. However, the Thai version incorporates the occasional military coup (they've had 18 since 1933). The most recent occurred in 2006. The majority had apparently grown weary of billionaire prime minister, and Man City owner, Thaksin Shinawatra's administration. When he was ousted, the Thai public took it in their stride and with some modicum of relief. Yet, when elections were held in 2007, Samak Sundaravej, a member of Thaksin's People Power Party, won a surprise victory.

One factor in Thaksin's undoing was his handling of the Malay insurgency that continues to stew in Thailand's three southernmost provinces. This insurgency has been characterised as a conflict between Buddhists and Muslims, but the mostly Muslim insurgents, who have been calling for Islamic law, have not been targeting their Buddhist neighbours. They have attacked police and army personnel, some of whom are rumoured to be involved in the drug trade, and relentlessly bombed government offices. The Thai military response has included village raids and a high-profile massacre of 32 insurgents, who were gunned down in a mosque. Unfortunately, the turmoil continues and Phuket has been receiving an influx of villagers from this region, which shows no signs of reconciliation.

Phuket is ruled by a provincial governor, appointed by the Interior Ministry in Bangkok, and three elected district councils: Thalang in the north, Kathu in the west and Muang in the south. However, the Nai Ampers (District Chiefs) are also appointed by Bangkok. The cities of Phuket and Patong have their own municipal governments, with elected city councils, the leading members of which serve as mayor. There are also elected provincial, district, and subdistrict (tambon) councils.

ENVIRONMENT

Phuket's rich and beautiful environment has been its own ecological undoing. Long before resort developers claimed the luscious west-coast beaches, tin miners raided Phuket's interior. When the pygmies roamed the forest, it didn't take a lot of digging to find metal. In fact, after the rains the tin practically surged to the surface of the soil. As a result, the now-extinct tribes are believed to have risen from the Stone Age before Europeans. They weren't alone in the jungle. Tigers, Malayan sun bears, rhinos and elephants once roamed the triple canopy rainforest.

Then the European tin-mining corporations built mining roads, harvested timber and tore through large swathes of soil. When the forest was gone, rubber plantations and fruit orchards were planted, which can make the interior feel cool and lush, but aren't Phuket's natural habitat. The last swathe of remaining rainforest is found in Khao Phra Thaew National Park (p114).

Rampant, unchecked development continues along the west coast. When Mom Tri built Club Med in Kata, he made sure the beach canopy remained intact. But most developers lacked his foresight and Patong is the worst example of unplanned development on the island. Now the east coast has become the new frontier for developers. This is alarming considering the mangroves, which are home to dozens of bird species, provide habitat for oysters and act as environmental filters for the Andaman Sea and have largely remained intact. If they begin to disappear, Phuket's ecology will be thrown even further out of balance and Ao Phang-Nga will pay the price.

Of course, the glorious yet fragile ecosystem of Ao Phang-Nga National Park (p128) is already threatened due to poachers who steal and sell eagles' nests and hunt monitor lizards in the *hongs* (caves semisubmerged in the sea) and powerful two-cycle speed boats that shuttle tourists to Ko Phi-Phi and spew oil into the sea. When you visit, the beauty will be so compelling you may not notice that the kingfisher population has suffered tremendously in the past few years. Kingfishers are an indicator species, and their absence does not bode well for Ao Phang-Nga's ecological health.

BOOKS & FILMS

Most of the relevant reading in relation to Thailand is set in Bangkok, although Alex Garland's riveting bestseller, *The Beach,* in which a backpacker utopia goes bad takes place on cliffside beaches of southern Thailand that recall the limestone islands in Ao Phang-Nga. The protagonist in Emily Barr's *Backpack* also tramps the budget trail through Thailand. *Travelers' Tales: Thailand,* compiled by James O'Reilly, makes some stops along the Andaman coast, and Philip Cornwel-Smith's *Very Thai* provides some sparkling insight into Thai pop culture.

Several Hollywood movies were filmed in and around Phuket. *The Man with the Golden Gun*'s legacy is still alive on James Bond Island in Ao Phang-Nga. Before Leonardo DiCaprio was a greenie he starred in the less-than-compelling adaptation of *The Beach,* during which national park beaches were redecorated with invasive tree species, so they would look more 'tropical'. Gotta love Hollywood. Most of the film was shot in Phi-Phi, but the Bangkok interiors were actually filmed in the OnOn Hotel in Phuket's Old Town. And portions of Robin Williams' classic *Good Morning Vietnam* were shot in Thalang.

If you're into Thai cinema, check out *OK Baytong,* an amazing story of a monk who leaves the monastery after his sister's mysterious death in southern Thailand. *Last Life in the Universe* pairs a suicidal Japanese man and a young, free spirited Thai woman together in Bangkok. *Satree Lek* (Iron Ladies) tells the true story of *kàthoey* ('ladyboy'; transvestites and transsexuals) volleyballers who won the Thai national championship in 1996. *Ong Bak* is a bloody *muay thai* (Thai boxing) martial-arts film.

DIRECTORY
TRANSPORT
ARRIVAL & DEPARTURE
AIR

Phuket international airport is situated at the northwest end of the island, 30km from Phuket City. It takes around 45 minutes to an hour to reach the southern beaches from here, and you could wait over an hour for the mythic metered taxis, which supposedly exist but are quite rare. The best bet is to hire a private car, which are widely available and cost 500B to 800B depending on your destination. Alternatively pay 120B and hop in a minivan destined for Phuket's Old Town, or 180B if you're headed to Patong, Karon or Kata. The minivans only leave when they have 10 passengers, so you may have to wait.

Thai Airways International (Map p39, A3; ☎ 076 211195; www.thaiairways.com; 78/1 Th Ranong, Phuket City) operates about a dozen daily flights to Bangkok (one way from 15,505B); it also has regular flights to/from 11 other cities in Thailand and international destinations, including Penang, Langkawi, Kuala Lumpur, Singapore, Hong Kong, Taipei and Tokyo.

Bangkok Airways (☎ 076 225033; www.bangkokair.com; 58/2-3 Th Yaowarat, Phuket City) has daily flights to Ko Samui (one way 1975B), Bangkok (one way 2725B) and Utapau for Pattaya (one way 3100B).

Nok Air (☎ 1318; www.nokair.co.th; Phuket international airport) links Phuket with Bangkok, as do **One-Two-Go** (☎ 1141, ext 1126; www.fly12go.com; Phuket international airport) and web-based **Air Asia** (www.airasia.com), from 726B one way. Air Asia also flies to Kuala Lumpur (one way from 1089B) and Singapore (one way 989B).

CLIMATE CHANGE & TRAVEL

Travel – especially air travel – is a significant contributor to global climate change. At Lonely Planet, we believe that all travellers have a responsibility to limit their personal impact. As a result, we have teamed with Rough Guides and other concerned industry partners to support Climate Care, which allows travellers to offset the greenhouse gases they are responsible for with contributions to energy-saving projects and other climate-friendly initiatives in the developing world. Lonely Planet offsets all staff and author travel.

For more information, turn to the responsible travel pages on www.lonelyplanet.com. For details on offsetting your carbon emissions and a carbon calculator, go to www.climatecare.org.

There are several international airlines with offices in Phuket's Old Town:

Dragonair (Map p39, D3; ☎ 076 215734; Th Phang-Nga)

Malaysia Airlines (☎ 076 216675; 1/8-9 Th Thungkha)

Silk Air (Map p39, D3; ☎ 076 213891; www .silkair.com; 183/103 Th Phang-Nga)

FERRY
During the high season, several boats ply the waters between Ao Ton Sai on Ko Phi-Phi and ports on Phuket. **Chao Koh Group** (☎ 076 246512) boats depart from Th Rasada, near Phuket's Old Town, for Phi-Phi at 8.30am, 1.30pm and 2.30pm and return at 9am, 2.30pm and 3pm (one way 400B). Get the going price before you turn up at the port, since touts here can charge up to double the real fare.

MINIVAN
Some Phuket travel agencies sell tickets (including ferry fare) for air-con minivans down to Ko Samui and Ko Pha-Ngan. Air-con minivan services to Krabi, Ranong and Surat Thani and several other locations are also available. Departure locations vary: see the **Tourism Authority of Thailand** (TAT; ☎ 076 212213; www.tat.or.th; 73-65 Th Phuket, Phuket City; ⏲ 8.30am-4.30pm) office. Minivans cost slightly more than buses, which all stop at the bus terminal in Phuket's Old Town.

VISA
Many Western nationals will be granted free entry for 30 days without a visa. See the **Ministry of Foreign Affairs Kingdom of Thailand** (www.mfa .go.th) website to check whether you must apply for a visa before arriving in Phuket.

ALTERNATIVE TRANSPORT OPTIONS
Phuket is an island, but that doesn't mean you have to fly here. If you're working to build the sort of climate-change karma points that would make Al Gore blush, take a bus from Bangkok (626B, 14 hours), Krabi (146B, four hours) or do the bus/boat combo from Ko Samui (494B, eight hours), which is linked to the gulf coast by a network of ferries. Speaking of ferries, you can take one to Phuket from Phi-Phi, Lanta and Krabi. Of course, you will probably choose to fly to Thailand from your home country, but you don't have to. The Port of Phuket is deep, and all manner of cruise ships and merchant vessels dock here. Why not take the slow boat?

GETTING AROUND
Phuket is quite large and local public transport leaves a lot to be desired, so most tourists hire cars (per day 1200B to 1500B) or motorbikes (per day 250B to 500B). Both are reasonably priced

and easy to find. All you need is a current driving license from your home country. Remember to keep it with you at all times, because checkpoints pop up – especially in Patong. Motorcyclists must wear helmets, and if you don't (which is monumentally stupid considering the prevalence of motorbike accidents in Phuket), you'll pay a fine.

There are regular săwngthăews, the Thai version of local buses, which run between resort areas and Phuket City. Most are converted trucks with bench seating in the beds. They're cheap, but can be packed and are very slow. A trip from Kata to Phuket's Old Town takes nearly two hours. On private transport you can get there in 20 minutes.

Taxis and túk-túks (motorised three-wheeled vehicles) are good alternatives, but they are surprisingly expensive. They don't have meters, so you should negotiate a fare before you leave. Most rides between resort areas cost at least 300B, and sometimes up to 500B one way. There's only a tiny price break for choosing a túk-túk over a much faster and safer automobile, so unless you crave the novelty ride (and you will…once) get in a car.

BOAT
Long-tail boats are easily hired on the beach for remote island and beach locations. There are also daily public boats to Krabi, Phi-Phi and Ko Yao, leaving from Ao Chalong and Bang Rong harbours.

CAR
Driving around Phuket looks complicated when you're bleary-eyed from a long flight, but it's a snap. The main roads are wide, the roundabouts are easy to manoeuvre and traffic snarls only occasionally. There are cheap car-hire agencies on Th Rasada in Phuket's Old Town near Pure Car Rent. Suzuki jeeps and Toyota sedans go for anywhere from 1200B to 1500B per day (including insurance), though in the low season the rates can come down to 750B. If you hire for a week or more, you'll pay near the low end of the range.

Some car-hire agencies sport international names like Budget, but if you book through an agent (rather than directly through the company), you must pay cash up front to receive the car, and the agency will usually bring the car to you. No matter which you choose, it's always a good idea to reserve in advance.

Andaman Car Rent (☎ 076 324422; www.andamancarrent.com; Moo 2, Cheangtalay, Thalang)

Budget (☎ 076 205396; www.budget.co.th.com; Phuket international airport)

Phuket New Car Rent (☎ 076 379571; www.phuketnewcarrent.com; 111/85 Moo 8, Th Tharua-Muangmai, Thalang)

Pure Car Rent (Map p39, C3; ☎ 076 211002; www.purecarrent.com; 75 Th Rasada, Phuket City)

Via Rent-A-Car (☎ 076 385718; www.via -phuket.com; 189/6 Th Rat Uthit, Patong)

SĂWNGTHĂEW & TÚK-TÚK

Large săwngthăew (literally two rows) run regularly from Th Ranong near the market to the various Phuket beaches for 40B to 70B per person. They operate from 7am to 5pm; outside these times you have to charter a túk-túk to the beaches, which will set you back 250B to Patong, 280B to Karon and Kata, and 340B to Nai Han and Kamala. For a ride around Phuket's Old Town, túk-túk drivers should charge 30B for an hour. You can also charter túk-túk between beach resorts. Rides cost 300B to 500B.

TAXI

If only Phuket had a fleet of metered taxis with published fares. Instead it has private cars, whose drivers can charge more for a 10-minute ride to Rawai from Kata than a 20-minute ride from Rawai to Phuket City. Don't try to make sense of it, just negotiate the fare before you leave. Rides generally cost 300B to 500B one way. Motorcycle taxis are much cheaper, and can cost as little as 30B per ride, but most work exclusively in Phuket's Old Town.

PRACTICALITIES
BUSINESS HOURS

In the high season, Phuket never stops doing business. Restaurants, unless they're serving breakfast, open at 10am and close at 11pm. Businesses and shops open at 8.30am and close at 6pm in Phuket's Old Town, and stay open as late as 11pm in the resort areas. Pubs, cafés and bars open at noon and close at midnight, and banks open from 9.30am to 3.30pm Monday to Friday.

DISCOUNTS

The Blue Card, a brainchild of the publishers behind the new *My Phuket Magazine,* is a free discount card distributed in the magazine. Buy the mag, get the card – it's that simple. It will fetch you discounts from 5% to 15% in a handful of retail shops and restaurants around Phuket. Log onto www.theblue card.com for more information.

ELECTRICITY

Thai electrical currents are 220V, 50 cycles. Wall outlets generally take the round, two-prong plugs, but some will also take the double-blade terminals, and the nicest resorts usually take both. It's always a good idea to grab an adapter from your home country if you can, but you can also find them in Phuket.

EMERGENCIES

Considering the amount of tourists and the volume of cash spent in Phuket, it's a wonderfully safe place. You will rarely feel uncomfortable or guarded, even in wild Patong. However, on the edges violence and crime do happen. The most common ambush spot is on Hwy 4233 between the Karon View Point and Rawai. In the past year at least four robberies have taken place where single motorbike drivers were pushed off their bikes and then robbed. One of the victims tried to fight back, and was stabbed to death. All of the attacks happened after midnight. If you're in a car, you have nothing to worry about, but motorbikers should double back to Hwy 402 if you need to head south from Kata or Karon.

Women sunbathing alone should also take care, especially on the remote northern beaches. During our research trip a 26-year-old Swedish tourist was raped and murdered on Hat Mai Khao in the middle of the day. In the crime's aftermath the TAT contemplated distributing whistles to women when they land in Phuket.

During the monsoon season the beaches in Phuket are far more dangerous than the people. An estimated 14 people a year (usually surfers) drown because of vicious rip currents on the west-coast beaches. Red flags are posted on beaches when the undercurrents are strong. If they're flying, stay out of the water. If you do get caught in a rip, don't fight it by swimming back to the beach. That's a good way to die. Instead swim parallel to shore. You will eventually elude its grasp and be able to make your way back to the beach, where you will probably have a long walk to your lounge. And remember to keep an eye out for jet skis when you're swimming outside the buoys.

But on the whole Phuket is very safe. During the high season the seas are tranquil, and the people are almost always warm and hospitable. Although hawkers and touts are ubiquitous, scams are extremely rare. They are just looking to make an honest deal.

If you do have an emergency, call the **police** (Map p39, C3; ☎ 191, 076 223555; cnr Th Phang-Nga & Th Phuket, Phuket City). If you need medical attention, contact the **Bangkok Phuket Hospital** (Map pp8-9; ☎ 076 254425; Th Yongyok Uthit, Phuket City) or **Phuket International Hospital** (Map pp8-9; ☎ 076 249400, emergency 076 210935; Airport Bypass Rd).

HOLIDAYS

New Year's Day 1 January
Chinese New Year (lunar) January–March
Magha Puja (lunar) January–March
Chakri Day 6 April
Songkran (lunar) April

Coronation Day 5 May
Visakha Puja (lunar) May
Asalha Puja (lunar) July
Khao Phansa (lunar) July
Queen's Birthday 12 August
Chulalongkorn Day 23 October
King's Birthday 5 December
Constitution Day 10 December

INTERNET

Wi-fi access is widely available in Phuket. Most hotels and guesthouses offer wi-fi connection for free to their guests, and several cafés and bars do the same. If you're travelling sans computer, it won't be hard to locate an internet café. They are everywhere and cost anywhere from 40B to 150B an hour. Check the following useful websites:

Jamie's Phuket (www.jamie-monk.blogspot.com)
Lonely Planet (www.lonelyplanet.com)
One Stop Phuket (www.1stopphuket.com)
Phuket Dot Com (www.phuket.com)
Phuket Gazette (www.phuketgazette.net)
Tourism Authority of Thailand (www.tat.or.th)

LANGUAGE

Thailand's official language is Thai. The dialect from central Thailand has been adopted as the lingua franca, though regional dialects are still spoken. Thai is a tonal language, with five tones. Written Thai is read from left to right. Transliteration of Thai into the roman alphabet renders multiple (and contradictory) spellings. After every sentence, men affix the polite particle *kháp* and women *khá*.

BASICS

Hello.	*sà·wàt·dee (kráp/ kâ)*
Goodbye.	*lah gòrn*
How are you?	*sà·bai dee rĕu?*
I'm fine, thanks.	*sà·bai dee*
Excuse me.	*kŏr à·pai*
Yes.	*châi*
No.	*mâi châi*
Thank you.	*kòrp kun*
That's fine. (You're welcome)	*mâi ฿en rai/ yin·dee*
Do you speak English?	*kun pôot pah·săh ang·grìt dâi măi?*
I (don't) understand.	*(mâi) kôw jai*
How much?	*tôw raí?*
That's too expensive.	*paang geun ฿ai*

EATING & DRINKING

This food is delicious!	*ah·hăhn née a·ròy!*
Please bring the bill.	*kŏr bin nòy*
I'm allergic to ...	*pŏm/dì·chăn páa ...*
I don't eat ...	*pŏm/dì·chăn gin ... mâi dâi*
meat	*néu·a sàt*
chicken	*gài*
fish	*฿lah*

GLOSSARY

ao – bay or gulf
hat – beach
ko – island
laem – geographical cape
moo – literally, 'group'; in this book it refers to a subdistrict
săwngthăew – common name for small pickup truck with two benches in the back; used as a bus/taxi
soi – lane or small street
thănŏn – street, road, avenue (we use the abbreviation 'Th' in this book)
túk-túks – motorised three-wheeled vehicles
wat – temple

EMERGENCIES

I'm ill.	chăn bòo·ay
Help!	chôo·ay dôo·ay!
Call ...!	rêe·ak ... nòy!
a doctor	mŏr
the police	đam·ròo·at

MONEY

The basic unit of Thai currency is the baht (B), made up of 100 satang. Notes come in 20B, 50B, 100B, 500B and 1000B. Coins are valued at 1B, 5B and 10B. Ask larger vendors or your hotel to break the 1000B notes. For exchange rates, see the Quick Reference inside this book's front cover.

You can do Phuket on the cheap or you can splurge like you're in Paris. It all depends on where you stay and what you eat. The minimum you can expect to spend is 1000B per day. That's if you stay in a budget hotel and eat local street fare. A more comfortable and reasonable amount is 3000B. Your room won't be outstanding, but you'll be able to include excursions and some nice dinners. If you're willing to spend up to 6000B per day, your trip will be full and memorable, and accented by dive trips and meals long enough to drain two bottles of red.

ATMs are everywhere and you won't have any trouble using your ATM or credit cards, which are a much better option than carrying cash or travellers cheques. Keep in mind that túk-túk drivers and small vendors don't carry change for anything over 500B.

NEWSPAPERS & MAGAZINES

The *Bangkok Post* (www.bangkok post.com) and the *Nation* (www .nationmultimedia.com) are Thailand's national English-language newspapers and are both a great read. The *Phuket Gazette* (www .phuketgazette.net) is the local English-language weekly. *My Phuket* (www.myphuketmag .com) is the island's new glossy, bimonthly mag.

DIRECTORY

TELEPHONE

You can tap into Thailand's mobile phone system in two ways. First, if you have a SIM-unlocked GSM 900-1800 compatible mobile phone, you can simply buy a Thai SIM card and over one hour of credit for 300B, then pay as you go. Or you can pay roaming rates on your home country-calling plan, which will have a Thai service agreement with a local network. If you do have a Thai mobile phone, calling internationally will be cheap and easy and you won't have to use those painful yellow pay phones. Just buy a Hatari Phonenet card at 7-Eleven for 300B and call the access number. The call won't drain any of your local phone credit and you can call most countries for 4B to 8B per minute.

COUNTRY & CITY CODES
Thailand (☎ 66)
Phuket (☎ 076)

USEFUL PHONE NUMBERS
Local directory inquiries (☎ 1133)
International direct dial (☎ 001)
Operator-assisted calls (☎ 100)

TIPPING

Tipping practices vary in Thailand. Expensive places add a 10% service fee and a 7% Value-Added Tax (VAT) to your bill. However, most restaurants do not. Service staff earn very low wages and always appreciate a little extra. When the service warrants it, tip liberally.

TOURIST INFORMATION

The **Tourism Authority of Thailand** (TAT; Map 39, C3; ☎ 076 212213; www.tat.or.th; 73-65 Th Phuket, Phuket City; ☷ 8.30am-4.30pm) has maps, information brochures and a list of standard săwngthăew fares to the various beaches.

TRAVELLERS WITH DISABILITIES

Given the narrow footpaths, the pace of traffic and very few adaptations, such as ramps, on the streets of Phuket, disabled travellers will have a fairly difficult time getting around by themselves. However, if you travel with a friend who can help you navigate the chaos on the streets, you'll have no trouble at all. If you are disabled and plan on travelling by yourself, the best bet is to hire a car with a driver who will make sure you get to where you want to go safely.

>INDEX

See also separate subindexes for See (p172), Do (p173), Shop (p174), Eat (p174), Drink (p176) and Play (p176).

000 map pages

INDEX

000 map pages

000 map pages